PRAISE FOR *IN SEASON*

"This devotional beautifully captures the heart of what sports can teach us, not merely about competition but about purpose, faith, and the strength of the human spirit. Elizabeth Laing Thompson thoughtfully weaves these themes throughout each devotion, using her gifts to encourage reflection, intention, and growth. Her words resonate deeply with my spirit and will undoubtedly inspire readers at every stage of their journey on the field and in life."

—**Jackie Joyner-Kersee**, six-time Olympic medalist

"I am so grateful for this book—it is much needed. We face so many things as female athletes, and having a book with encouraging tips and stories from female athletes who have been through some of the same experiences of these young athletes is so valuable. I wish that I had something like this growing up!"

—**Azurá Stevens**, WNBA basketball player for the Los Angeles Sparks; played college basketball at Duke University and the University of Connecticut

"I cannot emphasize enough how needed this book is. Elizabeth is someone whose writing I've relied on in specific phases of my life for its practical wisdom and spiritual direction. A book specifically helping young female athletes will truly be a blessing to so many young girls as they work to navigate the challenges of competing in their sport while trying to remain faithful to God."

—**Katie Chrest Erbe**, former Assistant Women's Lacrosse Coach at Army West Point and standout player at Duke University. A three-time All-American, two-time ACC Player of the Year, 2005 National Player of the Year, and six-time member of the US Women's National Team and 2009 World Champion.

"We were created to do life with others in order to live in its fullness! Elizabeth Laing Thompson pours wisdom into young women, which is essential for their ability to excel on and off sports fields. I wish I had a book like this when I was entering my high school and college seasons. These encouraging stories from other female athletes will remind young women that God can use them in unimaginable ways through the athletic opportunities He has given them."

—**Annabelle Hasselbeck**, host of Sports Spectrum's *What's Up* podcast; won two national championships in her career on the Boston College women's lacrosse team (2021 and 2024)

"What an incredible resource for young female athletes—I wish I'd had this much sooner in my athletic career! Competition and Christianity can be a confusing topic, but Elizabeth helps Christian girls navigate the unique challenges that we face both on and off the track and field. This book will give confidence and clarity to women who play sports and want to glorify God in the process."

—**Riley Knebes Muggler**, Oregon State Champion in 300m hurdles, University of New Haven NCAA Division II All-American, 2024 Olympic Trials qualifier

"I looked for a Christian devotional when my daughter was in high school where she can lean into God's Word to help her get through the challenges that she faces as an elite athlete. I was not successful finding anything. As a coach of high schoolers of all levels and as a mom of an elite athlete, this book is much needed and will help our teens mentally, emotionally, and spiritually! I have no doubt Elizabeth's book will meet a need of thousands of female high school athletes."

—**Beth Grace**, former collegiate athlete at UNC-Wilmington, assistant track and field coach at Coastal Christian High School, mother of an elite athlete

"She shoots . . . she scores! Elizabeth Laing Thompson's *In Season* is simply one of the best sports devotionals I've ever read. Elizabeth packs *In Season* with a winning blend of charm, humor, and practicality, bringing powerful spiritual truth into the locker room in a way that is highly relatable and encouraging. This is the devotional that every Christian female competitor needs."

—**Joshua Cooley**, Joshua Cooley, *New York Times* bestselling author and award-winning sportswriter/editor, whose sports books include *The One Year Sports Devotions for Kids, The Biggest Win*, and *Believe It: My Journey of Success, Failure, and Overcoming the Odds*

"This book will change the way girls see athletics and how they show up as athletes. Often, an athlete's humanity can become overshadowed by the winning and losing of contests, earning the approval of coaches, parents, officials, and peers, even making an idol of their talents. This book will keep girls from developing a perspective of their self-worth based on their athletic performance. Instead, they will have a GPS to establish and maintain their identity in Christ and allow sports to be an asset to their spiritual and emotional development."

—**M. Allison Murphy**, Ph.D., FACSM, EP, CSCS, NCAA Division I All-American hurdler, University of Pittsburgh Athletic Hall of Fame inductee, Masters Track and Field World Champion

IN SEASON

A 90-DAY DEVOTIONAL FOR FEMALE STUDENT ATHLETES
TO BUILD FAITH, STRENGTHEN CONFIDENCE,
AND TRAIN A GROWTH MINDSET

ELIZABETH LAING THOMPSON

ZONDERVAN®

FOR AVERY

ZONDERVAN

In Season

Published by Zondervan, 3950 Sparks Drive SE, Suite 101, Grand Rapids, MI 49546, USA. Zondervan is a registered trademark of The Zondervan Corporation, L.L.C., a wholly owned subsidiary of HarperCollins Christian Publishing, Inc. Requests for information should be addressed to customercare@harpercollins.com.

ISBN 978-0-310-17920-7 (audio)

Library of Congress Cataloging-in-Publication Data

Names: Thompson, Elizabeth Laing author

Title: In season : a 90-day devotional for young female athletes to build faith, strengthen confidence, and train a growth mindset / Elizabeth Laing Thompson.

Description: Grand Rapids, MI : Zondervan, [2026] | Audience: Ages 12 and up | Summary: "Discover your ultimate playbook for faith and athletics with In Season, a 90-day devotional for young female athletes. With interactive features such as goal setting, progress check-ins, reflection questions, and journaling prompts, In Season offers busy athletes everything they need to prioritize their spiritual growth while balancing their sport, academics, and relationships. No matter her athletic goals or level of play, every girl who competes in a sport faces similar joys and challenges throughout her athletic season: The excitement of competition. The sense of belonging. The pressure to win. The athletic season is a physical, emotional, and spiritual roller-coaster ride, and many girls feel so overextended and overwhelmed that they struggle to stay spiritually connected. In Season is a 90-day devotional that will meet girls where they're at. Tailored for young female athletes, each short devotion offers a much-needed spiritual perspective as readers navigate the highs and lows of sports and life, including building friendships and teamwork, developing leadership skills, cultivating a growth mindset, and more. With Scripture-infused reflections, real-life athlete stories, and practical exercises, In Season is intentionally designed to encourage resilience, confidence, and joy both on and off the field."-- Provided by publisher.

Identifiers: LCCN 2025047240 (print) | LCCN 2025047241 (ebook) | ISBN 9780310179184 hardcover | ISBN 9780310179191 ebook

Subjects: LCSH: Women athletes--Prayers and devotions--Juvenile literature | Christian athletes--Prayers and devotions--Juvenile literature | Athletes--Religious life | Sports--Religious aspects--Christianity | LCGFT: Devotional literature

Classification: LCC BV4596.A8 T466 2026 (print) | LCC BV4596.A8 (ebook) | DDC 242/.843--dc23/eng/20251229

LC record available at https://lccn.loc.gov/2025047240

LC ebook record available at https://lccn.loc.gov/2025047241

Names and some details have been changed in some illustrative examples to protect the privacy of individuals. In the case of the highlighted athletes' stories, experiences are recounted as accurately as possible according to their memories of the event(s) described.

Published in association with The Bindery Agency, www.TheBinderyAgency.com.

HarperCollins Publishers, Macken House, 39/40 Mayor Street Upper, Dublin 1, D01 C9W8, Ireland (https://www.harpercollins.com)

Cover design: Gabriella Wikidal
Cover illustration: Denise Plant

Printed in India City, Faridabad

26 27 28 39 30 31 32 33 / NT / 10 9 8 7 6 5 4 3 2 1

AUTHOR'S NOTE

Dear Friend,

I am so excited to share these devotions with you! As a former high school athlete, the wife of a former D1 quarterback, and mom of four teen athletes, this book is a deeply personal project. I know firsthand what sports can do for a girl's confidence and character, and I hope this book helps you thrive in your sport and in your faith.

The topics inside loosely follow what you may experience as your season progresses, but if you see a devotion that meets your need now, feel free to jump ahead. Each week's theme is introduced by a story from a real athlete's life. These ladies generously shared their hearts, and I'm thankful for their openness. I did my best to capture their experiences honestly. While I had to use some creative license in recreating and condensing a few events, or altering some details for privacy, the stories' overall spirit is true. Some of these athletes are competing at the highest level, and others are competing simply for the love of the game. (Find out more about them in About the Athletes!) In addition, the brief stories at the beginning of some devotions are either drawn from, inspired by, or adapted from experiences in my life and the lives of other athletes.

I pray these words help you walk closely with God and love your life as you navigate the joys and demands of your season. I'm cheering you on this season—and always.

Elizabeth Laing Thompson, June 2025

Preach the word; be prepared in season and out of season.
2 Timothy 4:2

CONTENTS

WEEK 10: HANDLING SPORTY FEELINGS

WEEK 11: REST AND TRUST

WEEK 12: FOR THE LOVE OF THE GAME

OVERTIME: BONUS MATERIAL

WEEK 1: IDENTITY

Time-Out: My Hopes, Prayers, and Goals for This Week

More Than This Sport: Elena's Story

Coach blew the whistle, signaling the end of soccer tryouts. Forty sweat-soaked, dirt-streaked girls milled around, nervously chatting. Waiting. Three days of tryouts, and it all came down to what Coach would say in the next five minutes.

Elena stood alone, pretending to stretch. Also pretending she was fine, like, *I'm definitely not freaking out even though I TOTALLY AM.*

She noticed Carly, another freshman, fake stretching nearby. Elena suspected Carly was also trying to hide an internal freak-out. Maybe they could pretend together.

"Hey, you did amazing work this week, Carly!" Elena called. "Your footwork is impressive. I'm sure you're going to make it."

"Thanks, I really want to make JV. But I didn't go to all the early morning preseason workouts like you did. You really put in the work," Carly said. "I bet you make var—"

"Stop! Don't say it!" Elena held up a hand, half serious, half laughing. "If you say it out loud, you might jinx it." Elena didn't really believe in jinxes, but she knew it was almost impossible for a freshman to make varsity.

But not *totally* impossible.

What if I make it? The hopeful thought zinged through her mind, filling her with a longing so intense it almost made her dizzy.

"Everybody line up on the field!" Coach then started calling names, sorting girls into groups of three, four, and five. "I'll call each group over and let you know as a group if you made JV or varsity—or if you're going home."

Hope and dread swooped through Elena's stomach as she watched group after group walk over to Coach. Some left whooping and high-fiving; others slumped off the field in silence. When Carly's group jogged away smiling, Elena felt a surge of happiness. Carly must have made JV.

"Elena, Kate, Rihanna!" Coach barked the names. "Come talk to me."

Elena and two sophomore girls jogged over to Coach. Behind her mirrored sunglasses, Coach's face was impossible to read.

"I'm sorry to tell you girls—"

Elena's hope plummeted.

"That you're going to have zero free time for the next two months, because you all made varsity."

Elena stared at Coach, blinking. Frozen. Had she heard her right?

Beside her, Rihanna and Kate were squealing and doing a complicated high-five dance.

Yes, she'd heard right. *Varsity!* Elena's heart set off a shower of happy fireworks. *I just made the varsity team. As a freshman!*

The next morning, Elena tried to pray for a few minutes before school, but thoughts about yesterday were still pinging around her head like flies trapped in a jar. *I am a varsity soccer player. I can't believe that's who I am.*

But then she had another thought: *Wait—playing soccer is what I do, not who I am. I am more than a soccer player. I am more than this sport. I need to remember who God says I am—what my real identity is.*

Elena opened her Bible and started searching for verses to help her remember.

THAT'S WHO YOU ARE

See what great love the Father has lavished on us, that we should be called children of God! And that is what we are!
1 John 3:1

WARM-UP

How do you describe yourself to other people?

Elena's revelation that morning was an important one. As thrilled as she was to make the roster and call herself a varsity soccer player, she recognized the temptation to make her sport her entire identity. That's what the world encourages us to do, isn't it? We tend to label people with identities based on the things they do.

She's an athlete.

An artist.

A bookworm.

An influencer.

Those labels aren't necessarily wrong or sinful, but when you become a Christian, you take on an entirely different identity. An identity that is infinitely more meaningful—and permanent. This week we're going to take a look at some Scriptures that describe exactly who we are as God's people.

One of the simplest—and most beautiful—verses is found in 1 John 3:1: "See what great love the Father has lavished on us, that we should be called children of God! And that is what we are!"

Let those words soak in for a moment: *Lavishly loved. Children of God. That is what we are.*

When you become a Christian, you become a daughter of God. A loved, saved, holy, blameless, adored, purpose-filled, Spirit-led daughter of God and follower of Jesus. You don't need the world's labels to feel good about who you are. You don't need your sport to feel confident, powerful, or worthy.

Because you are God's daughter, you have purpose and joy in your life, whether you make the team or not. Whether you are a starter or a supporting player. Whether you are a captain or a manager or a friend cheering from the bleachers.

You are more than your skills. More than your stats. More than your sport.

You are a daughter of God, and that never changes.

PRACTICE

We are loved, saved, holy, blameless, adored, purpose-filled, Spirit-led daughters of God and followers of Jesus. Which of these descriptions means the most to you, and why?

CHOSEN

But you are a *chosen people*, a royal priesthood, a holy nation, God's special possession, that you may declare the praises of him who called you out of darkness into his wonderful light.
1 Peter 2:9 (emphasis added)

WARM-UP

How do you feel when you are chosen? How do you feel when you're overlooked or ignored?

When Elena's coach chose her as a varsity soccer player, she felt amazing. Wanted. Valuable. That *chosen* feeling seeped into her heart, giving her an extra boost of confidence.

Scripture tells us that as Christians, we have been chosen by God. I picture it going like this: God looked out over the world and all its eight billion people, searching. Suddenly he stopped, his eye on *you*. He smiled, lifted an almighty finger, and announced, "I choose her."

God chose you to be *his*—his beloved daughter, his trusted representative.

In the apostle Paul's letter to the Ephesians, he expands on this idea, saying, "For he chose us in him *before the creation of the world* to be holy and blameless in his sight" (Ephesians 1:4, emphasis added). God didn't just choose you at the last minute because all the good players were gone and he was desperate to fill his team. God picked you before you were even born. Before the creation of the world. Somehow God, who exists outside time, knew you were coming into the world one day . . . and he picked you.

When you feel chosen like Elena did, it changes everything about how you see yourself. You feel important and valued. Confident and needed. You know you have something to give.

First Peter 2:9 explains that we were chosen for a purpose: "to declare the praises of him who called you out of darkness into his wonderful light." God didn't *just* choose you so you could walk around feeling good about yourself (though he does want you to feel confident and loved). He chose you so you could share that feeling with others. So you could shine a light back on him. So you could declare his praises, honoring him with your words and actions.

You won't always feel "chosen" in your sport. Sometimes you'll feel overlooked and unappreciated. You may experience seasons where you sit on the sidelines, feeling passed over and undervalued. But God will never fail to recognize your value. He'll never overlook you or forget to give you playing time. Yesterday and today and tomorrow and forever, God chooses you.

TAKE A KNEE

Father, thank you for picking me. Thank you for choosing me even with my imperfections and weaknesses. Please help me walk with godly confidence, bringing you glory and honor through my words and actions. In Jesus's name, amen.

THE ROYAL TREATMENT

But you are a chosen people, *a royal priesthood*, a holy nation, God's special possession, that you may declare the praises of him who called you out of darkness into his wonderful light.
1 Peter 2:9 (emphasis added)

WARM-UP

What is your favorite description in this Scripture?

Most sports divide athletes into various levels: junior varsity vs. varsity, select vs. premier. Like Elena, if you get chosen for a high-level team, you may experience a surge of confidence. You may be admired or even envied by others. You might even receive special privileges: maybe you get to wear the newest, coolest uniform or you receive extra coaching or you are invited to play in high-level tournaments or games.

As Christians, we qualify for unique privileges too. You might even say we receive "the royal treatment." When we fall in love with a king—King Jesus—he adopts us into his royal family and appoints us to priesthood.

In the Old Testament, Jewish priests had special responsibilities and access to God. A thick curtain in the temple kept worshipers out of the Holy of Holies, the place where God's presence resided. The Holy of Holies could only be entered once a year by one special person. On the Day of Atonement, the high priest would pass behind the curtain and into God's sacred presence. When Jesus died, that curtain ripped in two (see Matthew 27:51). Symbolically, this represented Jesus destroying the divide separating God from his people. Now, all Christians are royal priests who can enter the Holy of Holies to speak with God. We no longer need a mediator to speak to him on our behalf.

This season—and always—we can be as close to God as we want to be. Through prayer, we can "approach God's throne of grace with confidence" (Hebrews 4:16). We can ask God for whatever help we need—sports help, school help, relationship help. We can laugh with him and cry with him, go for walks and simply *be* with him.

It turns out the royal treatment is divine!

EXTRA REP

Here's another Scripture describing our priesthood: "And you are living stones that God is building into his spiritual temple. What's more, you are his holy priests. Through the mediation of Jesus Christ, you offer spiritual sacrifices that please God" (1 Peter 2:5 NLT).

LOSE THE HALO, KEEP THE HOLY

But you are a chosen people, a royal priesthood, *a holy nation*, God's special possession, that you may declare the praises of him who called you out of darkness into his wonderful light.
1 Peter 2:9 (emphasis added)

WARM-UP

How would you define the word *holy*?

Not only are we chosen, not only do we get to be royal priests—we are also part of God's holy nation. Let's unpack the word *holy*. As a kid, I always pictured holy people wearing white robes and glowing halos. Possibly strumming harps. Being holy meant you were so good that you were 99.9 percent perfect. *Holy* wasn't something I could ever be (or really wanted to be, if I'm being honest). But as my understanding of Scripture deepened, I learned that my definition of *holy* wasn't wholly right. (Thank goodness, because A) I'm not perfect, and B) it would be tough to compete in sports wearing a robe and halo.)

So what does it mean to be holy? For Christians, it means being "set apart." Elena and her friends felt "set apart" for something special when they made the varsity soccer team. Or you know those practices where Coach calls a few girls aside and gives them specific assignments? That's what God does with us; he calls us aside and says, "I have a job for you."

In a letter to his young disciple Timothy, Paul elaborates on this idea by comparing our work for God to work around the house: "In a large house there are articles not only of gold and silver, but also of wood and clay; some are for special purposes and some for common use. Those who cleanse themselves from the latter will be instruments for special purposes, made holy, useful to the Master and prepared to do any good work" (2 Timothy 2:20–21).

As God's holy people, we aren't meant for common tasks—we're not toilet brushes in the house of God. To prepare for our work, we first have to cleanse ourselves from worldly things. That means we won't always speak, act, or react like everyone else because God gives us different priorities and standards. We won't always fit in—because we're not supposed to.

Having a special purpose means that when you show up to practice, your coach has an agenda for you. It's the same when you're on God's team. You're not just there to do the drills and hone your skills—you're *also* there so God can touch others through you. Maybe he needs you to show kindness to a teammate, express gratitude to your coach, or model hard work and humility.

Your heavenly coach has set you apart for noble work, taking on special assignments in life and on your team. (No halo required!)

TAKE A KNEE

Lord, thank you for setting me apart for your purposes. Please help me honor you with my choices, and open my eyes to see the work you need me to do today. In Jesus's name, amen.

CALLED MEANS YOU HAVE A CALLING

But you are a chosen people, a royal priesthood, a holy nation, God's special possession, *that you may declare the praises of him who called you out of darkness into his wonderful light.*
1 Peter 2:9 (emphasis added)

WARM-UP

What's your favorite way to praise God?

We've talked about how God has chosen us, appointed us to his royal priesthood, and set us apart as holy. But *why* has God given us those identities? To make us feel happy and free? To help us feel good about ourselves, the way Elena felt after making varsity? Sure, God wants us to experience confidence, joy, and freedom in Christ—but there's more to it than that.

Your coach didn't pick you for your team just to make you happy—they picked you because you have something your team needs. They knew you could contribute. In a similar way, Peter says that God chose us and gifted us for a reason—so we "may declare the praises of him who called [us] out of darkness into his wonderful light." God called us to him, then gave us a new calling: to bring him praise, and to honor him with our words and our lives.

God deserves all the praise we can possibly give him, and it does our souls good to worship, but we also give him praise so others can hear how wonderful God is. Through us, they can see his love and mercy at work in our lives—changing us, healing us, giving us purpose. God doesn't just want us to keep those blessings to ourselves—he wants us to share them with others. When Jesus called his first disciples, he said, "Come follow me, and I will send you out to fish for people" (Mark 1:17). Following Jesus means sharing in his noble work. He came "to seek and to save the lost" (Luke 19:10), and we get to take on that great purpose, sharing our blessings and God's praise with others.

When Jesus chose you for his team, like a good coach he had a role already in mind for you. He blessed you that you might bless others. He called you, then gave you a calling.

PRACTICE

Whose life can you touch this week?

WHO'S YOUR MAN?

Christ will make his home in your hearts as you trust in him. Your roots will grow down into God's love and keep you strong. And may you have the power to understand, as all God's people should, how wide, how long, how high, and how deep his love is. May you experience the love of Christ, though it is too great to understand fully. Then you will be made complete with all the fullness of life and power that comes from God.
Ephesians 3:17–19 NLT

WARM-UP

Describe a time when you felt the love of God in an especially powerful way.

My daughter Cassidy had felt the basketball player's eyes on her all week in Calculus. Watching, winking, flirting from the desk directly behind hers. His attention mystified her: *We both play basketball, but that's where the similarities end.*

Friday morning before class, Cassidy was about to drop into her seat when he draped his long arms over the back of her chair, blocking her way. In a booming voice, he asked, "Cassidy, do you have a man?"

The room fell silent. The entire class turned to watch, wide-eyed. To her own amazement, Cassidy knew exactly what to say. In a loud voice of her own, she grinned and announced, "*Jesus* is my man."

The guy threw back his head and laughed. "Okay, I see how it is."

Cassidy sat down, smiling, to a chorus of friendly laughter.

Cassidy and Elena learned a similar truth from different experiences: The world encourages us to identify ourselves based on what we do—*I'm a varsity athlete*—and who we're "with"—*That's my friend group. My team. My boyfriend. They make me confident.* But when you become a Christian, God transforms your entire identity: Your new life is defined by, and led by, Jesus. He is your Lord and Savior—he is your man.

In Ephesians, Paul explains that Jesus makes his home inside us, guiding our choices, our actions, and even—as Cassidy experienced that day in class—our words. Our confidence no longer depends on unreliable, temporary things like social status, grades, appearance, athletic performance, or having a cool boyfriend. Our trust is in Jesus, the only man whose love never fails and never ends. His love is so wide, so high, so long, and so deep that it defies human comprehension. It's too ginormous for our little brains to grasp. But Paul assures us that the more we seek to understand and experience that love, the more complete we will become. Jesus fills up our empty spaces, our lonely places, with "the fullness of [his] life and power" (v. 19). He completes us.

We all want to feel a sense of identity, belonging, and connection, but know this: You already have the devoted love of the most amazing man who has ever lived. While your relationship with Jesus is not a romantic one, he can fill your heart completely with his perfect, faithful love. Now and always, Jesus is your man.

DRILL

Write down a few ways you have felt God's love recently.

____

____

____

____

____

____

____

____

YOUR REAL LIFE

For you died, and your life is now hidden with Christ in God. When Christ, who is your life, appears, then you also will appear with him in glory.
Colossians 3:3–4

WARM-UP

What makes you feel pressure in your sport?

Coach's expression was fierce, blazing around the circle at each player in turn. "I need your best. Your everything. For the next few months you eat, sleep, and breathe golf. Okay, yeah, do your homework or whatever. But besides that, no extras. No movies, no concerts, no coffee with friends. You can do those things after the season ends. Right now, golf is your life."

Part of Kenzie felt excited—*Yes, I'm all in, I'm ready to sacrifice, I know what it takes to win*—but her mind hiccupped on that last sentence: *Golf is your life.*

Is this sport really my entire life? she wondered. Where did God fit in during the season? Was God an "extra" she should set aside? That didn't feel right.

Today's Scripture reminds us what it means to give our lives to Jesus. When we become Christians, we die to our sinful selves and old ways, and God raises us to new life in Christ. Christ *becomes* our life, our everyone and everything. The center of our being, the guide for our decisions, our source of purpose, confidence, and joy. Our life is "hidden with Christ in God."

What does this truth mean for Christian athletes? It means that as much as we love our sport, we love God more. We are wholehearted about Jesus *and* sports—in that order. Sports require intensity, dedication, and sacrifice, and we give those things. We're passionate, committed, locked in. But we don't buy into the lie that insists we worship our sport as though it were our god.

As Elena reminded herself the day she made varsity, and Kenzie pondered during her coach's speech, sports is what we do, not who we are. It's our activity, not our identity. This knowledge keeps that part of life in perspective, even when others push you to obsess or excel to an unhealthy degree. You may feel enormous pressure from coaches, parents, your community, and even yourself. But today's verse keeps us grounded in God because it helps us remember, "This sport isn't everything. *Jesus* is my everything."

No matter how this season plays out, you'll still be God's daughter. You'll be chosen, royal, called, and holy. You'll have noble work to do, a special purpose in this world. Thanks to Jesus, you'll have an amazing—and meaningful—life in him.

PRACTICE

How can you keep God first in your heart this season? How can you create space for Jesus in your busy schedule?

WEEKLY CHECK-IN

What went well this week? What was hard? Did I meet the goals I set for myself?

How is my body feeling? How is my heart feeling? How do I feel about my connection with God?

In what ways do I need support? How can I invite that support?

What do I want to pray about for next week? Who can I invite to pray with me and for me?

WEEK 2: GROWTH MINDSET

Time-Out: My Hopes, Prayers, and Goals for This Week

I Call That a Win: Allie's Story

The start signal blew, and Allie dove into the pool for her heat in the fifty-meter freestyle. She barely felt the shock of the cold water—she was too busy hearing her coach's voice in her head: "You're going to have a breakthrough this meet, I can feel it."

Stroke, breathe, stroke, breathe.

Allie felt strong. She pictured her body as a blade slicing through the water.

Stroke, breathe, stroke, breathe.

Halfway there.

She executed the turn, pushing hard off the pool wall, zipping back the other way.

A burn started in her shoulders. Spread to her quads.

Her muscles were getting tired.

No! I'm not tired! Half a lap to go. I can push for half a lap.

The burn was reaching her lungs. She snagged one last gulp of air, put her head down, and sprinted to the finish. Her arms churned, her lungs screamed, her legs were on fire—

Her hand touched the wall.

Heaving for breath, Allie yanked the goggles off her head and looked up. Her coach stood at the edge of the pool, offering a disappointed, you'll-get-'em-next-time smile. She held up three fingers.

Third place in her heat? After all that? Third place wasn't good enough to get into the final.

Allie sank underneath the water in a cloud of bubbles, trying to hide her frustration.

She spent the rest of the meet cheering for her teammates, a tight smile stretched across her face. She didn't want to take away from her friends' victories, but by the end of the meet, she was exhausted from hiding her feelings.

On the drive home, her mom glanced over. "So . . . how are you?" Mom had that I-know-you're-upset gentleness in her voice.

Allie tried to disappear inside her hoodie, pulling the strings tight so most of her face was hidden.

"That good, huh?"

Allie made a snuffle-grunt-moan sound.

"Well, can I help you reinterpret your race?"

Allie emerged from her hoodie, fighting back tears. "There's nothing to reinterpret. Today was supposed to be my Big Breakthrough Race, but I didn't even make it into the final."

"But did you notice your *time*?"

Allie shrugged.

"You've been making steady progress, dropping time every meet. Today you shaved off a *whole second*. Allie, that's a huge PR! You can be so proud of that race."

"But my time wasn't good enough to even win my heat."

"Sweetie, you swam your best race ever. You can't control how fast other girls swim—all you can control is your own race. You did exactly what you were supposed to do, and I'm super proud of you."

Allie watched her town slip past the passenger window.

A whole second.

That *was* a lot of time in a fifty-meter race.

Maybe today had been a victory after all.

She half smiled at her reflection in the window. *Mom's right. I swam the race I set out to swim. I'm calling that a win.*

CHANGE YOUR MINDSET, CHANGE YOUR GAME

Finally, brothers and sisters, whatever is true, whatever is noble, whatever is right, whatever is pure, whatever is lovely, whatever is admirable—if anything is excellent or praiseworthy—think about such things.
Philippians 4:8

WARM-UP

How do you define success in your sport?

Allie needed her mom to help her think differently about her race. As Allie's mom pointed out, sometimes our definition of victory is too narrow. We downplay incremental progress because we're focused on one specific measure of success. We don't notice personal wins even when they're staring us in the face.

As we work on our mindsets this week, we're going to spend a few days exploring the apostle Paul's advice about cultivating a godly perspective. Paul said, "Whatever is true, whatever is noble, whatever is right, whatever is pure, whatever is lovely, whatever is admirable—if anything is excellent or praiseworthy—think about such things."

What do all these adjectives have in common? They're all *positive*. God wants us to intentionally set our thoughts on positive things, big and small, like:

- the *truth* that God's love never fails
- the *lovely* smile on your mom's face when she picks you up from practice
- the *admirable* way a teammate shows grace in a difficult conversation
- the *praiseworthy* service your youth group offers the local food bank

Focusing on the positive inspires gratitude, generosity, and joy. It transforms the way we experience the world. This perspective is not only an attitude-changer in life; it's a game-changer in athletics. Instead of subscribing to narrow definitions of success and failure, we can remember that some success can't be counted in time or statistics. For example:

- Maybe you didn't win, but you overcame a rough start. That's praiseworthy.
- Maybe you didn't get a PR, but you encouraged a teammate who did. That's admirable.
- Maybe you didn't start the game, but you contributed fresh legs when a starter got fatigued. That's noble.

With God, victory isn't just about wins and losses; it's about character, heart, and the way we represent Christ. The next time you compete, don't just focus on technique, stats, and outcomes; pay attention to your thoughts too. Your mindset matters. It might even change your game.

PRACTICE

Think about your next competition, then write down a definition for success that has nothing to do with time, statistics, or winning. For example: *It's a win if I stay positive the entire race.* Or: *It's a victory if the team works together selflessly and patiently.*

___

___

___

___

___

NO SUCH THING AS PERFECT

Fix your thoughts on what is true, and honorable, and right, and pure, and lovely, and admirable. Think about things that are excellent and worthy of praise . . . Then the God of peace will be with you.
Philippians 4:8–9 NLT

WARM-UP

How would you define perfectionism? In what ways are you a perfectionist?

"Amazing race, Cameron . . . Congrats, Cam! . . . Best race yet!"

A swarm of supporters showered Cameron with compliments as she sat down to take off her spikes. She smiled, pretending to appreciate their encouragement. But the words bounced off her—Cameron didn't believe a single one.

I didn't deserve the time I got, she thought. *I was slow out of the blocks. And those last two hurdles were sloppy. I have so much work to do.*

Maybe you know a Cameron—or maybe you *are* a Cameron. Cameron is a perfectionist. She isn't happy unless she has done everything perfectly. Every. Single. Itty. Bitty. Thing. Not surprisingly, Cameron is rarely happy with her performance. Not even when she wins a race. Not even when everyone tells her she did a good job. Like Allie, Cameron is getting hung up on the wrong details and failing to see the bigger picture.

Let's take a second look at Philippians 4:8–9, the passage we explored yesterday. First, let's think about what Paul *didn't* say: "Fix your thoughts on your weaknesses. Focus on your flaws. That's the only way to grow. Don't get complacent. Never settle for less than perfect."

Um, no. Paul teaches that God wants our thoughts fixed on

positive things, true things, beautiful things. He wants us to hunt for excellent things that deserve praise. When we fix our thoughts on what's good, Paul promises we'll find God's peace.

What might this positive perspective look like in a sports setting? In Cameron's case, it might sound like this: *Those last two hurdles were rough, but I cleared them. That's a win! My start was slower than usual, so I'll keep working on that. If I improve my start and my stamina, maybe next time I'll shave off even more time. But I made progress today, and I'm happy with that.*

Do you see the difference? A positive mindset doesn't mean we ignore mistakes or areas where we hope to grow, but neither do we ignore our victories. As Cameron and Allie are both learning to do, we search for progress and celebrate it. We find the good, the lovely, the admirable, the praiseworthy—even in mediocre or "bad" performances.

Perfect is an impossible standard and an unhealthy mindset. When we embrace God's way of thinking, not only do we experience more of his peace and presence, we also find more joy in life—and in sports.

DRILL

Write down something positive you did in your last practice or competition.

THE MENTAL GAME

The weapons we fight with are not the weapons of the world. On the contrary, they have divine power to demolish strongholds. We demolish arguments and every pretension that sets itself up against the knowledge of God, and we take captive every thought to make it obedient to Christ.
2 Corinthians 10:4–5

WARM-UP

Spend a few minutes focused on positive, thankful thoughts. How does that brief exercise affect your mood?

Ninth Grade Me crouched on the edge of the court, waiting for the ref to wave me into the basketball game. My thoughts whirled:

I hope I get to take a shot.

Who am I kidding? I don't want the ball—I never make baskets!

The whistle blew, the ref waved, and with negative thoughts still pummeling me, I stumbled into the game.

Games may appear to be won and lost during competition . . . but honestly? They're usually won and lost inside our heads.

Every time you step into competition, you probably have a thousand internal voices shouting for attention. Just as Allie recalled her coach's words during her race, you may hear your coach's voice, reminding you what to do. If your sport is technical, you're probably talking yourself through each micro-step of your skill. And then there's the voice of your confidence. On rough days, your "confidence" might be saying mean things like:

You're not prepared. You should have practiced harder.

That girl you're guarding? She's way better than you.

You're sloppy and slow.

Negative thoughts often shout the loudest, don't they? They discourage us, even insult us. They exaggerate our weaknesses, downplay our strengths, and undermine our confidence.

The Bible calls our enemy, Satan, "the accuser" (Revelation 12:10).

Satan loves to whisper false accusations, and sometimes he tells lies that make us insecure and hesitant. But God gives Christians a set of "weapons" to help us fight our spiritual and mental battles, and these weapons have power to tear down anything Satan builds. In 2 Corinthians 10:5, the apostle Paul writes, "We take captive every thought to make it obedient to Christ."

Picture negative thoughts as the devil's cruel minions attacking our confidence, relationships, and joy. (Of course, not every unwanted thought comes from the devil, but he does like to attack our peace of mind.) Whenever negative thoughts show up—whether they come from our own insecurity or self-doubt, or from some other place—God can help us take those thoughts captive, slapping them in handcuffs and sending them away.

Say you have a thought like this: *I always mess up that play—I'm so stupid!* To battle that thought, first take it prisoner by identifying it as a dishonest intruder. Then use the "weapon" of truth to rewrite it: *I have messed up that play a few times, but I'm not stupid. I do other things well. I'll keep working on that play, but in the meantime, I'm going to lean into my strengths.*

By rewriting that negative thought, you take charge of your mental game. You expose the exaggeration as a lie, reclaim your confidence, and remember that God is with you. And that's a victory.

DRILL

Write down a negative thought that sometimes pops into your head when you're training or competing. Then rewrite that thought with a positive, God-centered, solution-oriented perspective.

Negative thought:

____

Positive rewrite:

____

THE HARDEST IT WILL EVER BE

Consider it pure joy, my brothers and sisters, whenever you face trials of many kinds, because you know that the testing of your faith produces perseverance. Let perseverance finish its work so that you may be mature and complete, not lacking anything.
James 1:2–4

WARM-UP

What's the toughest thing you've faced so far this season?

My daughter Avery shuffled into the house after practice, letting her gear clatter to the kitchen floor before slumping down beside it.

I paused mid-carrot chop. "I take it your first preseason workout was a little rough?"

"Yeah, but it's okay," Avery said, a glint of determination flashing in her eyes. "Today is the worst I'll ever feel. Tomorrow I'll be in better shape than I was today, then the day after that I'll be even stronger, and I'll keep getting better every day. Today is the hardest it will ever be." She grinned, heaved herself up off the floor, and stole a carrot.

Sports require perseverance. Perseverance means we hang in there even when it's hard—*especially* when it's hard. Like Avery, we don't give up after a tough workout, even if we feel embarrassingly out of shape. Perseverance means we don't get down and think, *I'll never catch up, so I might as well give up*. Like Allie, we acknowledge progress even if we're not yet where we want to be. We don't get discouraged—we get determined.

The Bible has a lot to say about perseverance. Today's passage is a little confusing the first time you read it: "Consider it pure joy . . . whenever you face trials"? *Really, God? You want me to be* happy *when life is hard?* Yes. Yes, he does. Sort of.

When we face adversity, we cultivate perseverance. And perseverance is an essential character trait God uses to work on us—and in us. When we persevere through difficulties, we mature our faith, strengthen our character, and cultivate a growth mindset.

Sports work the same way, don't they? We have to stretch our limits if we want to improve. If we don't push hard in the weight room, we don't get stronger. If we don't go all out during sprints, we don't get faster. Without perseverance, we'll just stay the same. We won't experience the satisfaction and thrill of growth.

Motivated athletes learn to embrace challenges, to view them as opportunities for improvement. Motivated athletes don't shy away from hard workouts or sit out the tough games. Their attitude is, "Bring it. Adversity makes me better."

When we persevere today . . .

Tomorrow's faith will grow a little stronger.

Tomorrow's character will become a little more mature.

Tomorrow's sprints will be a little faster.

No matter how hard today feels, it pays to persevere, because today is the hardest it will ever be.

DRILL

Look back on a challenge you've overcome in the past. How did you grow through it? Journal a few thoughts in the space below.

____

____

____

____

____

____

____

SETBACK? OR OPPORTUNITY IN DISGUISE?

Consider it pure joy, my brothers and sisters, whenever you face trials of many kinds, because you know that the testing of your faith produces perseverance. Let perseverance finish its work so that you may be mature and complete, not lacking anything.

James 1:2–4

WARM-UP

What do you think it means to persevere?

Yesterday we looked at James 1:2–4, which encourages us to grow through trials. Today let's focus on verse four: "Let perseverance finish its work so that you may be mature and complete, not lacking anything." What's perseverance? It's toughness. Endurance. The ability to keep going when others might give up. To keep going when *you* want to give up.

God uses perseverance to help us mature. To complete his work on our character. To help us become stronger, better, more humble versions of ourselves. That sounds great, right? When I hear that, my first thought is, *Yay, sign me up for perseverance! I'd like to grow into a stronger version of myself.*

But perseverance, by definition, isn't fun. You can't *persevere* without going through something difficult, something you'd rather avoid. Like getting third in your heat, not making the final despite giving your all. Or not making the starting lineup and spending most of your time on the bench. Or rehabbing an injury instead of competing.

I don't think this passage is suggesting we sit around hoping for adversity to come our way, but it is offering us an empowering perspective: Tough times aren't all bad news. They have silver linings.

Adversity forces us to persevere, and if we let perseverance do its work, it deepens our character and maturity.

That means setbacks are also opportunities. They pave the way for different kinds of growth: Growth in perseverance. Character. Knowledge. Skills. Strength. Relationships. Leadership. Mental toughness.

Maybe you aren't playing because your coach doesn't think you're ready. That stinks, but it's okay. How can you use this time to *get* ready? Can you train hard while you wait your turn? Watch the starters, listen to the coaches, and grow your knowledge of the sport?

Maybe an injury has you sidelined. That stinks, but it's okay. What skills can you work on while you heal? How can you contribute to your team even when you're not playing?

Setbacks don't have to set *you* back. With the right mindset, they can set you on a path toward growth and new opportunities.

TAKE A KNEE

Dear God, thank you for loving me enough to push me out of my comfort zone. Thank you for trusting me to handle setbacks with courage and resilience. Please give me strength to grow, and show me the opportunities hiding amid the difficulties. In Jesus's name, amen.

NEXT PLAY

Not that I have already obtained all this, or have already arrived at my goal, but I press on to take hold of that for which Christ Jesus took hold of me. Brothers and sisters, I do not consider myself yet to have taken hold of it. But one thing I do: Forgetting what is behind and straining toward what is ahead, I press on toward the goal to win the prize for which God has called me heavenward in Christ Jesus.
Philippians 3:12–14

WARM-UP

Do you consider yourself resilient? Why or why not?

The softball sailed high, a moon shot. Bella followed it, tracking its arc, squinting in the afternoon sun. *Yes.* Finally, some left field action.

She jogged forward, eyes never leaving the ball. Sheesh, the sun was bright! Bella's eyes burned, but she didn't blink, couldn't risk losing the– *Where is the ball?* Her vision filled with white-hot sun.

The ball plopped to the ground.

Oh. There it was.

Bella scooped it and lobbed it to second, knowing she was too late. She yelled at the sky, furious with the sun—and herself. From the dugout, Coach's voice boomed, "Next play, Bella!"

Bella took a deep breath and thumped a fist into her glove.

Reset.

Ready.

If you play your sport for a few days, you're going to make a few mistakes. If you play your sport for a few seasons, you're going to make a *lot* of mistakes. And your ability to recover from those mistakes is going to have a huge effect on your performance—and your happiness.

Let's revisit Paul's letter to the Philippian church, a letter known for its and-the-crowd-goes-wild level of joy. You might assume Paul wrote this exuberant letter while vacationing in the ancient equivalent of a gorgeous beachside resort, but no. He was wearing chains, in prison for preaching the gospel (see (Philippians 1:7, 13).

How did Paul stay upbeat and keep going day after day? He chose not to linger in the past: "Forgetting what is behind and straining toward what is ahead, I press on toward the goal to win the prize for which God has called me heavenward in Christ Jesus" (v. 14). Chains or no chains, Paul still had sermons to preach, churches to encourage, souls to save. He chose to keep pressing forward—*straining* forward—into greater righteousness. Greater growth.

What might that kind of mindset look like for us?

We trust God's forgiveness when we sin, embracing his grace (1 John 1:9).

We face disappointments with resilience, trusting God's plans for our future (Romans 8:28).

We don't waste game time beating ourselves up—we reset for the next play.

Paul teaches us to learn from our past without living there. Our goal isn't to avoid *making* mistakes—it's to *recover quickly* from mistakes. To use them as springboards into growth. As Paul might say, "Forget what is behind; strain toward what is ahead." In sports, we would say, "Next play."

DRILL

The next time you make a mistake in your sport, challenge yourself to reset quickly for the next play.

THE STUFF YOU CAN'T CONTROL

Peter asked Jesus, "What about him, Lord?" Jesus replied, "If I want him to remain alive until I return, what is that to you? As for you, follow me."
John 21:21–22 NLT

WARM-UP

In what areas are you most tempted by comparison?

Peter denied the Lord three times on the night Jesus was arrested. It was a devastating failure in Peter's leadership and an even more devastating betrayal of their friendship. In John 21, after Jesus's death and resurrection, he gave Peter three opportunities to express his love and devotion, a chance to redeem those denials and start fresh in their friendship.

At one point in the conversation, Jesus hinted that one day Peter would be arrested and killed, just as Jesus had been. Not loving this news, Peter pointed at one of the other disciples and asked, "What about him, Lord?"

Jesus responded simply: "If I want him to remain alive until I return, what is that to you? As for you, follow me."

We don't have control over many things in our lives, including our own futures. We don't know what God has in store. The misty future is filled with question marks: *Are college sports in my future? What career will I build? When will I fall in love?*

And then there are the smaller questions, the right-now questions. We may be tempted, as Allie was after her swim meet and Peter was during his conversation with Jesus, to compare our lives to others': *Why does that skill come naturally to her when it's so hard for me? Why did Coach give her the start instead of me? Does God have something good in store for me?*

In moments of uncertainty, Jesus's perspective can be helpful. In saying, "What is that to you?" he is reminding Peter: *Keep your eyes on your own life. Don't worry about others, or about a future you can't control.* Then he gives Peter a job: "As for you, follow me."

We too can follow Jesus's advice to Peter, keeping our eyes on our own lives. We can focus on our own roles and responsibilities, the assignments Jesus has given us.

As Allie's mom reminded her, we can't control what a competitor or teammate does or what a coach decides. We can't control factors like who's taller than us, the level of talent in the next lane, or whether a college coach likes the way we compete. As you head to practice today, focus on the things you *can* control, like your attitude and effort. And remember, you are only in charge of yourself.

As for you... just give your best. That's the best you have to give.

PRACTICE

We can control our attitude and effort. Which area do you want to focus on today, and why?

WEEKLY CHECK-IN

What went well this week? What was hard? Did I meet the goals I set for myself?

How is my body feeling? How is my heart feeling? How do I feel about my connection with God?

In what ways do I need support? How can I invite that support?

What do I want to pray about for next week? Who can I invite to pray with me and for me?

WEEK 3: SPIRITUAL HABITS

Time-Out: My Hopes, Prayers, and Goals for This Week

Jincy lugged her gear through the ice rink's double doors—her bag was always heavy, but today it seemed to weigh a thousand pounds. She dressed in silence, not in the mood to chat with teammates. Not in the mood to play hockey. Not in the mood to do anything.

As she slumped onto a wooden bench and began wrestling her feet into skates, her friend Kate plopped down beside her. Kate nudged Jincy in the side with an elbow. "You okay?"

"I'm exhausted," Jincy said. "I guess the busyness of the season's really getting to me. I can't snap out of it."

Kate studied her friend through a squint-eyed gaze. "How's your walk with God going?"

"My huh?" Jincy squinted back at her friend, confused. Being tired didn't have anything to do with God or faith. Shouldn't Kate be asking about her sleep schedule or vitamin intake or something?

"You're a Christian," Kate said, "so how's your walk with God? You know, prayer? Bible study?"

Despite the chill in the rink, Jincy felt a warm flush creep into her cheeks. "I've been kinda busy," she mumbled.

Kate nodded. "I get it. This season has been crazy for me too. But God is where our energy comes from. Where our life comes from." She paused, tugging on a tangled skate lace. "Hey, do you know the passage in Ezekiel about the bones coming back to life?"

Jincy felt a half smile pulling at her lips. "Are we talking Bible story or zombie apocalypse movie?"

Kate laughed. "It actually would make an epic movie scene. So God shows the prophet Ezekiel a vision of a bunch of dry bones lying in the desert—it's like, these aren't just dead people, they're *extra* dead. God tells Ezekiel that the dry bones represent people whose strength has gone and hope has dried up because they have been depending on themselves instead of him. But then God breathes life into the bones and turns them into a mighty army, ready to serve him."

"Interesting story, cool movie idea, but . . . what does that have to do with me being tired?" Jincy asked, double-knotting her laces.

"Without God we're nothing but dry bones—no energy, no life," Kate replied. "But when we walk closely with God, he gives us *his* life and power. He breathes them into us. *God* is where our energy comes from."

"Dry bones pretty much describes the way I've been feeling," Jincy said. "It's been more than just physical tiredness—I've felt uninspired about everything, even hockey. I guess that's what happens when I run on my own energy instead of depending on God."

As they stood and headed for the ice, Jincy felt a small flame of conviction light inside—the desire to change.

Before entering the rink, Kate turned and gave Jincy's shoulder pad a friendly punch. "You've got this. Reconnecting with God really will help you feel different—it's just a matter of finding time for him."

"*Stealing* time feels more like it," Jincy said as they glided onto the ice. "But I know you're right, and I'm going to make time for God. Thanks for calling me out."

"Anytime. Now let's get these dry bones of ours moving around the rink before Coach gives us extra laps."

TRAINING IN RIGHTEOUSNESS

All Scripture is God-breathed and is useful for teaching, rebuking, correcting and training in righteousness, so that the servant of God may be thoroughly equipped for every good work.
2 Timothy 3:16–17

WARM-UP

What character trait would you like to strengthen?

You spend a lot of time training for your sport: working out, doing drills, building strength and muscle memory. The more you train, the better prepared you are.

God wants Christians to engage in another kind of training—training in righteous living. Just as we don't automatically know everything about our sport, we don't automatically know how to walk with God. We have to learn how to have a relationship with him: how to pray, read his Word, and apply it to our lives. This week we're going to explore the power of daily spiritual habits like Bible study and prayer. We'll also explore strategies for maintaining those habits even when the sports season grows hectic.

As Kate reminded Jincy, spending time with God isn't just one more overwhelming to-do we cram into our packed schedule; it's the practice that makes all the other to-dos doable! Bible study and prayer fuel our spiritual energy, equipping us to live the life God wants. The apostle Paul shared similar thoughts in a letter to his young disciple Timothy, explaining that reading Scripture does many things for us: It teaches, challenges, corrects, and trains our hearts in righteous living.

You've probably noticed that righteous living, aka godly behavior, doesn't always come naturally. In fact, sometimes God's ways are the exact *opposite* of our instincts:

- We want to be self-sufficient, but God calls us to lean on him for strength (Jeremiah 17:5–8).

- We love comfort, but Jesus calls us to deny ourselves (Luke 9:23–26).
- We naturally put our own interests first, but God calls us to put others first (Philippians 2:3–4).

We don't master spiritual habits like these overnight—we grow into them over time. Just as you've spent years honing your athletic skills, improving little by little, day by day, so spiritual training takes time. Focus. Effort. Repetition.

And what is the end goal of that growth? Paul says it is to be "thoroughly equipped for every good work." God has assignments for us, good things he needs us to do, tasks that accomplish his purpose in this world. Now that's an exciting training plan!

TAKE A KNEE

Father, thank you for caring about our character and progress. I love growing closer to you and stronger in my faith. Please equip me to accomplish the tasks you have set aside for me. In Jesus's name, amen.

FINDING A ROUTINE DURING THE SEASON

In the morning, LORD, you hear my voice; in the morning I lay my requests before you and wait expectantly.
Psalm 5:3

WARM-UP

When it comes to your weekly schedule, are you naturally a planner or a "pantser" (a person who flies by the seat of their pants)?

"Elizabeth, I want to talk about your eating plan for the meet tomorrow."

I looked up from my homework to find my dad standing over my desk. "My . . . eating plan?"

Dad flashed his trust-me smile. "I've been reading about metabolic surges. Here's what I want you to try . . ."

I'm happy to tell you that my well-meaning dad cared enough to make a race-day "eating plan" for his daughter. I'm sorry to tell you that plan involved eating a Snickers bar twenty minutes before a 1600-meter race. I'm even sorrier to tell you I came in last place. (Thank you, bad food science.)

As misguided as Dad's metabolic surge theory was, he was right about this: Proper nutrition takes planning. And as a Christian athlete, you need more than just a healthy diet; you also need spiritual nourishment if you don't want to feel like a sack of dry bones stumbling around. Staying spiritually nourished during the hectic sports season takes three things: intentionality, consistency, and creativity.

Intentionality means making a plan. Can you establish a routine for spending time with God each day? Set a realistic goal you can pull off even on the busiest of days: five minutes, ten minutes, fifteen minutes.

Next step: *When* will you spend that time? We're more likely to spend time with God when we are *consistent*—when we pray and read God's Word at a similar time each day. Then it becomes a habit, and we don't have to remind ourselves to do it. Today's Scripture from Psalm 5 gives us a peek into David's routine: Every morning before his day got going, he went to God. Morning times with God don't work for everyone, but they do have a few advantages:

- We can invite God into our day before it gets started.
- If we wake up feeling anxious, we can hand our worries over to God first thing.
- We can step out to face the day's challenges feeling connected to God.

If you are barely able to form coherent sentences before school, a morning routine may not be the best fit for you. You might have to be *creative* to figure out a time that works.

This week, I invite you to take time to choose a routine for your walk with God for the rest of your season. Find a rhythm that works, a plan that brings you joy. Then wait in expectation for your Dad in heaven to draw near.

PRACTICE

Once you come up with an idea for a routine, share it with a spiritual friend or mentor. Ask them if they think your plan is realistic and if they have any other suggestions. Once you feel happy with your plan, you might also consider inviting them to check in to see how it's going.

SHORT AND SWEET

And when you pray, do not keep on babbling like pagans, for they think they will be heard because of their many words. Do not be like them, for your Father knows what you need before you ask him.
Matthew 6:7–8

WARM-UP

On a scale of 1–10, how comfortable do you feel praying?

A few weeks into the lacrosse season, my daughter Avery and I were doing dishes together after dinner. "I feel disconnected from God," she said, aggressively scrubbing a pot. "I've had zero free time, and I can't figure out when to read my Bible and pray."

We spent the next three pots brainstorming, finally settling on a ten-minutes-a-day-with-God plan. Avery must have felt better because she started being nicer to the pots.

Sound familiar? During the season, your day probably goes something like this:

1. Get up before dawn, still sore from last night's game.
2. Shovel food into your mouth, obsessing over what Coach might say at practice.
3. Quickly do something with your hair.
4. Pack a lunch, your backpack, and a thousand pounds of gear.
5. Pull out your Bible to read—*Oh, crud, I was too tired to do homework last night—just kidding, no time for a devotion. I have to do that assignment.* Say a quick, regretful prayer: *I'm sorry, God, I'm so overwhelmed, Please help me make it through today.*
6. Do school for eight mind-numbing hours.
7. Rush to practice, give it your all.
8. Inhale a late dinner.
9. Do homework for two hours before falling asleep on your desk.
10. Wake up hours later, wipe drool off your desk, and finally crawl into bed.

I'm tired just reading that list. Let's all go take a nap. (Not that you have time for a nap.)

When you're in season, staying connected to God can feel like one more to-do you don't have time to do . . . even if it's a to-do you really *want* to do. (Try reading that ten times fast!) Both Avery and Jincy *wanted* to stay close to God during their seasons, but finding time was challenging. During hectic times, we can take comfort from Jesus's words in Matthew 6: "You won't be heard because of your many words . . . your Father knows what you need before you ask him."

Is God angry or disappointed when our prayers are shorter than usual? No.

Will he choose not to bless your sports season because you skipped some morning devotional times this season? Absolutely not.

The point is not how long we pray every day—the point is *that* we pray in some way every day. That we find a moment to connect with our heavenly Father. Maybe that means . . .

- Setting your alarm five to ten minutes earlier so you can pray briefly before school.
- Praying on the drive to school.
- Taking a prayer walk around the block when you get home.
- Sitting outside for a few minutes each evening to tell God about your day.
- Journaling a prayer in bed before you fall asleep at night.

Long prayers aren't necessarily the best prayers. If all you have time for today is a brief connection—a "Hi, God, it's me. I love you and need you"—that's okay. Even if your prayer time is short, he's there for you, ready to listen, ready to love you.

PRACTICE

When can you find a few minutes to pray today?

BREATH PRAYERS

The king said to me, "What is it you want?"
Then I prayed to the God of heaven, and I answered the king, "If it pleases the king and if your servant has found favor in his sight, let him send me to the city in Judah where my ancestors are buried so that I can rebuild it."
Nehemiah 2:4–5

WARM-UP

Do you think long prayers are more valuable than short prayers? Why or why not?

High School Me collapsed onto the couch beside my mom as she was folding laundry.

"Something bothering you?" she asked.

"Mom, the cross-country schedule is killing me. I really needed to talk to God today, but I couldn't find a single break during the day."

Mom set a towel aside. "Grab my Bible and open it to Nehemiah—I want to tell you about 'bullet prayers.'"

Yesterday we talked about the value of spending brief but consistent time with God, and how short daily prayers can keep us connected during busy seasons. (We also saw that my girl Avery and I had similar struggles in high school!) But what about days when we don't have even a few minutes to spare, and yet we desperately need to connect with God?

During my junior year of high school, my mom introduced me to today's passage. It's about an Israelite named Nehemiah who served the Persian king. The Jewish people had spent decades living in exile. Although some Jews had returned to Israel to rebuild, Nehemiah learned that the walls of Jerusalem, the city where God's temple used to be, still lay in ruins. Heartbroken, Nehemiah spent days mourning, begging God for the chance to go home to help rebuild.

When the king asked Nehemiah why he looked sad, Nehemiah knew it was his Big Moment. His chance to ask the king to send him home. He had already spent days praying about this, but here in the crucial moment, Nehemiah wanted to connect with God again. To draw God's special attention to the conversation. So Nehemiah threw another quick prayer heavenward—the prayer must have taken the space of a single breath—and then made his bold request. The king said yes.

My mom called Nehemiah's faster-than-fast prayer a "bullet prayer"; I call it a "breath prayer." Like Nehemiah, we don't always have time to drop to our knees, but we can still send up quick prayers asking for God's presence, guidance, and favor. As Jesus taught us yesterday, the length of our prayers isn't what's important—*faith* and *relationship* are what matters. God is ever-present and attentive, a devoted Father. And when his children ask for help, he always listens.

DRILL

In the years since her conversation with Kate, Jincy has learned to incorporate breath prayers into her workouts. She does it like this: As she inhales during an exercise, she says, "Father." As she exhales, she says a one-line prayer like, "I trust you" or "Be with me." Try saying a breath prayer in a moment of need today.

MAKING SPACE FOR GOD

Very early in the morning, while it was still dark, Jesus got up, left the house and went off to a solitary place, where he prayed. Simon and his companions went to look for him, and when they found him, they exclaimed: "Everyone is looking for you!"
Mark 1:35-37

WARM-UP

How do you feel about the idea of spending a longer time in prayer?

Have you ever wished you could spend a day with Jesus? If you read Mark 1:21-39, you can—sort of. In these verses, Mark describes everything Jesus did for about twenty-four hours. Reading about Jesus's day is both amazing and exhausting—Jesus was a busy and extremely selfless person.

First, Jesus preached a sermon at a Sabbath service. Afterward, he went to Simon Peter's house for lunch, but when they arrived, Peter's mother-in-law was sick, so Jesus healed her. Then Jesus spent the afternoon with Peter's family. After sunset, things got hectic again. The entire town showed up at the door, begging Jesus to heal all who were sick.

And so he did. Person after person arrived trembling and ill, then left healed and happy. As the moon rose high and the night wore on, what tears of joy and hugs of gratitude must have filled that little house! When the last person danced their way home, I picture Jesus collapsing into a borrowed bed, weariness in his bones but a contented smile on his face.

After all that exertion and socialization, you might expect Jesus to sleep late the next morning, but nope. Jesus got up before sunrise and slipped away to spend time alone with God. As soon as the town awoke, they interrupted his prayer time, and he got back to work serving others.

How did Jesus have the strength and energy to serve so many people day after day? I think this early-morning moment gives us a big clue: Jesus drew strength from his walk with God. From his prayer life.

We've been talking about the power of short prayers. But perhaps, like Jesus, you can also make space for some longer times with God. Times when you can pray unhurried. When you can talk to God about school, stress, sports . . . everything.

Like Jesus, you might have to get creative. Maybe one morning you get up while the world is still dark and quiet. Maybe one weekend you take a prayer walk and pour out your heart to God, or you take your Bible and prayer journal to a coffee shop. Or maybe you sit outside and listen to worship music as you admire God's creation.

Sprinkling some longer prayers in alongside the short ones adds depth to your walk with God. The longer conversations help forge a connection that sustains you even on busy days when you're sprinting full steam ahead.

PRACTICE

Get out your calendar and find a day when you can spend a longer amount of time with God. Write it down and plan how you'd like to connect with him.

SECRET STASH SCRIPTURES

How can a young person stay on the path of purity? By living according to your word. I seek you with all my heart; do not let me stray from your commands. I have hidden your word in my heart that I might not sin against you.
Psalm 119:9–11

WARM-UP

What's your favorite Scripture?

Confession: I have a secret chocolate stash. In a drawer beside my bed, I hoard a few bars of my favorite treat: Ghirardelli dark chocolate with sea salt caramel. Every night, I eat two (cough—maybe three) squares as I sip Sleepytime tea and read before bed. I hide that chocolate because it makes my taste buds sing hallelujah and I don't want my family snarfing it. I hide that chocolate so I can fully savor it in peaceful moments.

I also have special "drawers" in my heart where I store my favorite Scriptures. Each verse offers a taste of God's wisdom, power, and truth. Each one has a depth of meaning worth relishing, a richness that sets my heart singing.

Psalm 119 eloquently describes the beauty of God's Word. It celebrates the ways it enriches our heart, protects us from poor choices, and equips us to live our best life. When we store God's Word deep in our heart, it protects us from missteps and guides us toward wise decisions, reminding us of God's will and his ways.

When you're in season, you probably don't have the luxury of doing a lengthy Bible study session every day. But that doesn't mean you can't dwell deeply in Scripture. By tucking a few favorite passages into your heart, storing them in your memory bank, you can meditate on them whenever you want to. They'll be ready and waiting whenever you need their guidance. Ever since Kate encouraged Jincy to reconnect with God, Jincy has memorized many Scriptures, and she often recites them during workouts as a way of bringing God into her day. For example, during timed sprints, she might challenge herself to recite a verse as many times as she can before the timer sounds.

Here are a few dark chocolate passages you might add to the secret drawer of your heart:

"Love the Lord your God with all your heart and with all your soul and with all your mind and with all your strength" (Mark 12:30).

"Be strong and courageous. Do not be afraid; do not be discouraged, for the LORD your God will be with you wherever you go" (Joshua 1:9).

"The LORD is compassionate and gracious, slow to anger, abounding in love" (Psalm 103:8).

Why not choose one "secret stash" Scripture to hide in your heart today?

DRILL

Choose a Scripture to memorize this week and write it in the space below.

WITH YOU

I will give you every place where you set your foot, as I promised Moses. . . . Have I not commanded you? Be strong and courageous. Do not be afraid; do not be discouraged, for the LORD your God will be with you wherever you go.
Joshua 1:3, 9

WARM-UP

Where is it easiest for you to sense God's presence? Where is it most difficult?

When practice ended, High School Me dumped my backpack into my mom's minivan and collapsed into the passenger seat. "Everything okay?" Mom asked in a worry-tipped voice.

I grunted and switched the AC to Arctic Blast. "I just felt so . . . in the world all day, you know? All the gossip and complaining and gross jokes floating around . . . I felt like God was a million miles away."

Ever felt that way at school? At practice? In the locker room? Like you're immersed in situations where God feels far away and faith seems like a barely there memory?

In the book of Joshua, the people of Israel were about to cross the Jordan River and enter the promised land. Although God was giving this land to his people, it was still occupied by pagan nations. The Israelites were entering new lands with different customs, and they were preparing to fight battles for God. Isn't that how it feels stepping out into the world sometimes? Like you're entering a foreign place where you don't belong—a place where God's ways are strange (or even despised) and you have to fight to remain righteous?

As the Israelites prepared to cross the river, God offered them a bright promise: "I will give you every place where you set your foot. . . . The LORD your God will be with you wherever you go."

You and I share in this promise because when we become Christians, God's Spirit comes to live inside us (1 Corinthians 6:19). The spiritual habits of prayer and Bible study are ways we invite

God into our daily life, and they help us maintain a strong sense of his presence everywhere we go. But God isn't just with us during our devotional times—his Spirit lives within us *all* the time. Like the Israelites who crossed the Jordan, we take God with us wherever we go. Everywhere we set our feet—every place we walk, run, train, play, or pray—God goes with us.

Today and every day, no matter where you go or what the world throws at you, you can take each step with courage and confidence, because God is with you.

TAKE A KNEE

Lord, thank you for being with me everywhere I go. Please give me wisdom in tricky situations, courage when I need to be different, love for those who don't know your ways, and comfort knowing you are with me. In Jesus's name, amen.

WEEKLY CHECK-IN

What went well this week? What was hard? Did I meet the goals I set for myself?

How is my body feeling? How is my heart feeling? How do I feel about my connection with God?

In what ways do I need support? How can I invite that support?

What do I want to pray about for next week? Who can I invite to pray with me and for me?

WEEK 4: COACHABILITY

Time-Out: My Hopes, Prayers, and Goals for This Week

We Did It: Hannah's Story

Why am I doing this to myself? Hannah thought, tossing a pole onto the grass in her backyard with a grunt of frustration. *I'm already having success in high jump and long jump—why would I want to start at square one with pole vault? Flinging your body into the air is . . . slightly insane. Definitely dangerous. And ridiculously technical.*

But she knew why—it was because her mom had vaulted in college and had offered to help Hannah learn.

Hannah picked up the pole and tried a few more swing drills in the grass. Everything felt awkward, unnatural. After a few more sloppy jumps, she wiped sweat from her forehead, then made a deal with herself: *I'll give it a month. I'll let Mom coach me, and if I don't start getting the hang of it, I'm going back to jumping, where I belong.*

Hannah spent the next month biting her tongue as her mom taught her the basics of pole vault. Doing the same drills over and over (and over and over) again. Getting comfortable with making a thousand mistakes every practice. Swallowing her pride every time Mom had to correct her form. Retraining her perfectionist brain to embrace failure as part of the learning process.

Somewhere around week three, something Mom said clicked. This time when Hannah vaulted over the practice bungee, it felt like flying. Hannah wasn't sure who was prouder—Hannah or her mom. And just like that, Hannah fell in love with pole vaulting. Another month passed, and Hannah didn't even notice—she was too hooked to quit vaulting.

Fast-forward two years, and Hannah was at the Reno Pole Vault Summit, competing alongside the top vaulters in the nation. As she warmed up, she spotted Becky Holliday walking over to her pit, and a shimmery feeling set Hannah's stomach swirling. *Becky Holliday! Silver medalist in the 2012 Olympic Trials! And I get to learn from her today!*

Then Becky said, "Okay, Hannah, show me what you've got."

Hannah jumped, her mom filmed, and then they listened

as Becky dissected Hannah's run, plant, and form. "You need to raise your right shoulder—get that arm as high as possible to elevate your plant. Like this," Becky demonstrated.

Hannah studied her form, imitated the move.

"Better," Becky said. "Now let's see it in a vault."

Hannah vaulted, focusing on her right shoulder positioning, and right away, something shifted. Her vault angle felt different. She flew over the practice bungee, landed on the mat, and sat up to see Becky and her mom beaming. "Yes!" Becky said. "Do that tomorrow and watch what happens."

The next day, at the competition portion of the summit, all Hannah thought about was Becky's coaching: *Raise your right shoulder, raise your right shoulder.* It became an internal chant.

Hannah opened at 13 feet—and cleared it by a mile.

Next she attempted 13'6"—no problem.

Then her personal record, 13'10"—easy.

The bar went up to 14 feet.

Hannah's stomach went swirly. Fourteen feet—the height she needed to clear if she wanted to go to the next level. The height she'd been dreaming of for two years. The barrier that separated elite high school vaulters from very good ones.

She started her run, hearing Becky's voice in her head—*raise your right shoulder, raise your right shoulder*—planted, flew into the air . . .

and cleared fourteen feet.

As Hannah lay on the mat, grinning at the sky, she heard her mom and Becky whooping with excitement. Hannah sprinted over to hug them.

"Way to go!" Becky offered a high five.

"You did it!" Hannah's mom's cheeks were flushed with joy.

"*We* did it," Hannah corrected. "I never would have cleared that height without your coaching. Thank you both so much!"

TRUST THE PROCESS

Anyone who rebukes a mocker will get an insult in return. Anyone who corrects the wicked will get hurt. So don't bother correcting mockers; they will only hate you. But correct the wise, and they will love you. Instruct the wise, and they will be even wiser. Teach the righteous, and they will learn even more.
Proverbs 9:7–9 NLT

WARM-UP

What's the strangest drill a coach has ever made you do?

It's not easy to learn a new skill or sport. Like Hannah did with pole vaulting, you have to silence your inner perfectionist and embrace the eating-humble-pie learning process. The same holds true when you join a new team and you have to embrace a different culture, new expectations, or a different role.

And what about those brain-bending times when a coach wants you to unlearn a familiar skill? To start from scratch and do things a new way? The unlearning-relearning experience can be difficult—even embarrassing.

You might get worse before you get better. Way worse.

You might wonder whether your coach is nuts or just mean.

You might feel offended and question what your coach is telling you. *I'm already a good player. I've been doing fine the old way—why is she messing with my groove?*

Or you might feel insecure and question yourself. *Do I even know how to play this game? Should I just give up?*

The book of Proverbs offers practical wisdom for times when we're in Learning Mode. Today's verse says, "Instruct the wise, and they will be even wiser. . . . Teach the righteous, and they will learn even more." It's surprising to note that this passage is about teaching people who are *already* wise and righteous. You might think that wise, righteous people are done learning, and now they can just coast, relying on their past success. But this proverb reveals that wise people can grow even wiser. Righteous people can become even more righteous.

In the same way, maybe you are already a great athlete—or at least a promising one. Your existing skills and game IQ have taken you far. But if you want to become even better—hit a dream PR, make an elite team, win a title—there's always room to grow.

Our past success can either be a springboard into future growth or a limiting factor. We may be tempted to think we've got everything figured out, but Proverbs reminds us that even the wise, righteous, and successful can continue growing. So if a coach or mentor wants to teach you a new approach, it can't hurt to listen and learn. Like Hannah, if you embrace the coaching, you might experience a breakthrough. In time, you might even become better, stronger, or faster than you thought possible. You just have to trust the process.

DRILL

Journal a brief response to this question: How has coaching made you better?

HOW TO BE A WISE ~~GUY~~ GIRL

But correct the wise, and they will love you. Instruct the wise, and they will be even wiser. Teach the righteous, and they will learn even more.
Proverbs 9:8–9 NLT

WARM-UP

What's the best advice you've ever received?

"I'm doing lots of work outside of practice, Coach," Emory said proudly. "Daily sit-ups and push-ups, Sunday runs . . . I'm not taking a single rest day!" She paused, ready for one of Coach's rare compliments.

Instead, Coach said, "Emory, I want you to stop the Sunday runs. The sit-ups and push-ups you can keep, but only two days a week. Overtraining is unwise—you're going to get injured."

Emory's jaw dropped. "But I thought I was doing the right thing!"

"Too much of the right thing can be a bad thing. Trust me."

Today we're taking a second look at Proverbs 9. We might think being wise means we know everything and have nothing left to learn, but this passage tells us different: "Correct the wise, and they will love you. Instruct the wise, and they will be even wiser." Gaining wisdom begins with knowing that we *don't* know everything, then looking for opportunities to grow.

Let's translate that biblical wisdom into sports wisdom:

Wise athletes aren't complacent, convinced they've already mastered everything.
Wise athletes trust their coaches enough to try things a new way.
Wise athletes embrace correction and constructive criticism.

Emory had great intentions with her hardcore workout plan, but her coach knew better, and Emory helped herself by listening.

Hannah was already having success vaulting, but she was eager to grow. When Becky Holliday critiqued her form, Hannah didn't hang her head in embarrassment—she learned. And just like today's proverb predicts—"Correct the wise, and they will love you"—both Emory and Hannah appreciated the coaching.

Humility and coachability don't always come easily. We may have to swallow our pride and trust others. But the more we grow, the wiser we become, and the wiser we become, the more we grow. The more we grow, the more we appreciate the ones who helped us get there. It turns out being a wise ~~guy~~ gal is a smart goal.

PRACTICE

What's one way you can demonstrate wisdom this week?

LISTEN FIRST, TALK SECOND

My dear brothers and sisters, take note of this: Everyone should be quick to listen, slow to speak and slow to become angry, because human anger does not produce the righteousness that God desires.
James 1:19–20

WARM-UP

What's your first response when you feel criticized?

"Sunita! Off the field now! Kat—you're in for Sunita."

Sunita grudgingly left the game and jogged over to her coach.

"What was that?" Coach's eyes were angry slits. "You should have passed—Mia was wide open. That shot was a rookie move."

Defensiveness bubbled up inside Sunita, hot and angry. *I didn't see Mia. And I would have made that shot if the sun hadn't been in my eyes.*

The words were already climbing up Sunita's throat, but Coach was still talking, so Sunita swallowed hard and tried to listen.

Like Sunita, when we feel criticized or attacked, our first instinct is usually to defend ourselves: *But you don't understand . . . Let me explain what I was thinking . . .*

It's not fun admitting we made a mistake or realizing we have room to grow. Everything in us wants to justify our decisions, make ourselves look good, and prove we were right all along. The moment we feel criticized, we may get offended and feel embarrassed, singled out, and stupid. We may also feel hurt and angry. We can get defensive, so busy trying to explain ourselves that we can't hear one word our coach is saying.

Today's reading from the book of James advises us to do the exact opposite of our natural inclination: Listen first. Talk later (like, way later). Don't give in to anger.

Why? Because anger doesn't bring about the righteousness God desires. When we're angry—especially defensive-angry—think about what happens:

- We may mouth off to a coach or referee. (We all know how fantastic *that* goes.)
- We may make hotheaded comments we don't actually mean.
- We may hurt our relationships with coaches or teammates.
- We may undercut our example for Christ on our team.

The next time you receive some criticism or coaching that's tough to swallow, try following James's advice: Pretend your mouth has a pause button, and listen before you speak. When it's your turn to respond, instead of firing off excuses or disagreement, try asking questions instead:

- *Can you help me understand what you mean?*
- *Can you give me another example?*
- *Can we go over that play again?*

Asking questions gives us an opportunity to listen, time to calm down any unruly emotions, and a moment to wrap our heads around the advice we've been given.

Listen first. Talk later. Stay cool. You'll avoid an argument, and you might just learn something.

TAKE A KNEE

Lord, thank you for the Bible's wisdom and for the chance to continue growing as a player and a person. Please give me the self-control to listen before I speak and the humility to learn from constructive criticism. In Jesus's name, amen.

THE EMBARRASSMENT EXPRESS

If you reject discipline, you only harm yourself; but if you listen to correction, you grow in understanding.
Proverbs 15:32 NLT

WARM-UP

How would you decorate for a pity party?

"Vivian, what are you doing?" Daila's shout sounded annoyed.

Vivian froze, letting the volleyball hit the floor. She stared at the senior captain, confused. "What's wrong?"

"Your body positioning is wrong," Daila said. "You should be facing the passer."

Vivian's face burned. She swallowed the words she wanted to say—*Give me a break, I'm new to this position*—and said, "Sorry, I didn't know."

"Well, now you know," Daila said, smacking Vivian's arm in a shake-it-off gesture. "Let's try again."

Have you ever hurt yourself by rejecting a correction? I totally have. When someone corrects me, my first response is to feel stupid: *I should have known that.* From there, the I-feel-stupid emotional train ride has two stops: Embarrassment and Defensiveness. If I stop the train at Embarrassment, I obsess over people's opinions: *Now they think I'm an idiot.* I may throw myself a pity party complete with black balloons and streamers. (This is not a fun party.)

If I travel farther down the line to Defensiveness, I start trying to prove I wasn't wrong after all—or even if I *was* wrong, it wasn't *my* fault I was wrong: *You should have told me that before. I didn't know!* We should also note that defensiveness can take two forms: Bruce Banner Mode and Hulk Mode. Bruce Banner mumbles grumpy objections under his breath. The Hulk gets angry and smashy. Either way, defensiveness is counterproductive because we waste time arguing instead of growing. We hurt ourselves by missing out on a chance to learn, and if we don't watch our words, we may also hurt other people's feelings.

Every athlete has gaps in their knowledge, skills, and experience at some point, and Proverbs 15:32 offers us a way out of embarrassment when those gaps come up. The proverb teaches us a growth mindset that is encouraging and even empowering. It reminds us that rejecting discipline slows down our progress, but accepting correction makes us better. Just as Vivian learned from a teammate, and Hannah embraced coaching from her mom and from an expert, we too can learn from others. We can view every mistake as a chance to improve—to "grow in understanding." To add to our knowledge, skills, and experience. This perspective transforms the way we receive correction:

- Instead of, *I'm such an idiot*, we think, *That's one less mistake I'll make tomorrow. Future Me will know better.*
- Instead of, *Everyone thinks I'm dumb*, we remind ourselves, *Everyone else had to learn that lesson at some point just like I did.*
- Instead of, *I should have known better*, we remember, *I just haven't learned that yet.*

The next time someone corrects a mistake you've made, don't catch a ride on the Embarrassment Express. Instead, thank them for helping you grow—because now you know.

DRILL

Rewrite this negative thought with a growth mindset:
I'm the only one on the team who hasn't mastered that skill.

____

____

____

IMAGINARY CRACKERS

Follow my example, as I follow the example of Christ.
1 Corinthians 11:1

WARM-UP

Who do you admire on your team and why?

I heard footsteps on the trail behind me and eased over to let the faster runner pass. Instead, she fell into step beside me. I recognized Karen, one of the best runners on our cross-country team.

"You're doing great," she said. "You just need to relax your upper body."

"Huh?" I could hardly eke out the one syllable—meanwhile I'd witnessed Karen belting out Broadway melodies without breaking stride.

"You're wasting energy," Karen insisted. "Stop making fists, and—this sounds weird, but it works—pretend you're holding a cracker between your thumb and fingers. Then brush your imaginary crackers against your hips as you run."

Feeling dumb, I unclenched my fists and pressed my fingertips around pretend crackers. Karen grinned at me. "Perfect. I learned that trick at running camp. It saves energy, I promise!" She sped off to join the faster girls. I clutched my pretend crackers and tried to keep up.

Coaching comes in many forms, and the best coaching doesn't always come from an official coach. If we keep our minds and hearts open, we can pick up tips from teammates and others in our sport. As a new runner, I had never been to a running camp, but I still benefited from a friend's camp experience. And as we saw for Hannah, some of the most valuable coaching she ever received came from a successful vaulter she met at a summit.

Paul's first recorded letter to the Corinthian church offers practical guidance for new believers learning to follow Christ and build a healthy church family. He concludes one section with a simple invitation: "Follow my example, as I follow the example of Christ." As Paul learned from Christ, so the Corinthian disciples learned from Paul. In a similar way, you and I can seek mentors in our sport and in our faith—people who model Christlike lifestyles.

God sent Jesus to earth to model obedience, submission, and love. When we recall Bible stories about Jesus, we can ask ourselves the famous question "What would Jesus do?" But it's also helpful to learn from Christians who do daily life with us. We can watch and listen as they navigate difficult conversations, or offer someone forgiveness, or pray faithfully through stressful situations. Their example teaches us how to apply faith to our own daily context.

People who keep learning keep growing. This holds true in our faith walk and in our sports: Athletes who learn the most grow the most. And just as Jesus isn't the only godly example we have to follow, so coaches aren't the only people worth learning from. We can pick up inspiration, knowledge, and strategies from teammates—even from competitors.

It's been years since Karen gave me that tip, but to this day I pinch imaginary crackers between my fingers when I run. Every time, I remember my friend with a smile.

DRILL

Whose example are you following in your faith walk? Who are you learning from athletically besides your coaches?

___

___

___

___

___

TWO UNDERRATED WORDS

Then I acknowledged my sin to you and did not cover up my iniquity. I said, "I will confess my transgressions to the LORD." And you forgave the guilt of my sin.
Psalm 32:5

WARM-UP

How do you feel when someone apologizes to you?

The pitch went wild—wide and high. So high the batter nearly did a backbend trying to avoid decapitation.

At first, the batter looked furious, ready to hurl her bat aside and storm the mound. Her teammates in the dugout already had legs straddling the wall, ready to run out and defend her. But then the pitcher thumped her chest and shouted, "My bad! I'm sorry!"

The batter tapped a finger to her helmet and nodded as if to say, "Apology accepted. Forget it." And just like that, the tension dissipated. The batter reset, and the game resumed.

Two of the most underrated words in sports—and life—are two of the hardest words to say: "I'm sorry."

I'm sorry requires courage. It feels embarrassing and vulnerable to admit a mistake instead of shifting blame.

I'm sorry requires humility. It means owning our error. We don't point the finger, make excuses, or tack a *but* onto the end of the apology.

I'm sorry paves the way for forgiveness and a fresh start. It allows the other person to let the thing go more quickly. They don't have to harp on what we did wrong because we already see it. We're working on it. And it's hard to stay mad at someone who is already apologizing.

We see this truth played out in today's verse, where the psalmist confesses and acknowledges his sins, then receives swift forgiveness from God. When we sin against God or other people, we find freedom and grace in confession. When we lose our temper, speak thoughtless words, or behave selfishly, *I'm sorry* makes a big difference.

Making an athletic mistake isn't a sin, but *I'm sorry* is helpful in sports too. No athlete is perfect. We all have off days and bad starts. We forget plays and compete distracted. We miss cues and bumble steps, drop passes and fumble batons. The more quickly we say "I'm sorry," the more quickly everyone moves on. We bypass time-wasting behaviors like blame-shifting and finger-pointing. We sidestep excuses and arguments. We move directly into the productive part, where we correct the problem.

The next time you mess up, don't panic, beat yourself up, or deflect responsibility. Just say, "I'm sorry." When you see how quickly everyone forgives and moves on, you'll experience the true power of two underrated words.

DRILL

How do you feel when you need to apologize?

WHEN YOU HAVE CONFLICT WITH A COACH

Since a king's word is supreme, who can say to him, "What are you doing?" Whoever obeys his command will come to no harm, and the wise heart will know the proper time and procedure. For there is a proper time and procedure for every matter, though a person may be weighed down by misery.
Ecclesiastes 8:4–6

WARM-UP

What's the toughest conversation you've ever had with a coach?

Mari lingered after cheer practice, taking her time packing up. Watching Coach out of the corner of her eye (but pretending she wasn't watching). Waiting to catch her alone.

The longer Mari waited, the more butterflies joined the swarm already in her stomach. She kept imagining the look on Coach's face when Mari asked for the chance to be a flyer instead of a spotter. Would Coach be annoyed? Angry? Or open to something new? Mari took a deep breath. *You've been praying about this conversation. Don't chicken out now.*

Every athlete has a few tricky conversations with coaches. Maybe, like Mari, you want to ask for more responsibility or opportunity. Or maybe you feel insecure and want to ask if the coach is upset with you. (Or maybe she's *definitely* upset with you, and you need to clear the air.) And maybe, like Hannah, your coach is your mom or a person you have a relationship with outside your sport, which adds an extra layer of complexity to the dynamic. These difficult conversations require courage, wisdom, and a bit of planning.

Ecclesiastes offers a wealth of insight for complicated situations. The author, traditionally considered to be King Solomon, can come across as cynical, but he shared realistic wisdom for navigating complex social-emotional dynamics. In chapter 8, Solomon offered advice for dealing with authority figures. He began by saying, "Since a king's word is supreme, who can say to him, 'What are you doing?'"

It's difficult to question authority figures, isn't it? In Solomon's day, the big authority was the king; in your life, the big authorities are probably parents or guardians, teachers, and coaches. Your coach has the right to decide All the Things for your team: playing time, roles, strategies. And most coaches don't appreciate players questioning their choices or methods.

Solomon went on to say, "Whoever obeys his command will come to no harm." This observation probably holds true on your team: When you do things Coach's way, Coach stays happy. Things go smoothly. Nobody gets hurt.

But what about times when you need to speak up about a problem or concern? Solomon wrote, "There is a proper time and procedure for every matter, though a person may be weighed down by misery." When you feel "off" with a coach, it's a heavy burden—like walking around with a squat bar strapped to your shoulders.

As stressful as it is to feel tension with your coach, Solomon suggested we wait for the right *time*. In a sports context, that means praying for wisdom (and perhaps seeking advice from mentors) about when to bring up an issue.

Sports bring up strong emotions, and some conflict is inevitable. But when we seek advice, pray for guidance, and approach issues wisely, we can address conflict and find resolution on the other side.

TAKE A KNEE

Father, I feel burdened by a tough conversation I need to have. Please provide the right opening for the conversation, and please give me the courage and wisdom I need to communicate well. Thank you for wanting to help me find peace. In Jesus's name, amen.

WEEKLY CHECK-IN

What went well this week? What was hard? Did I meet the goals I set for myself?

How is my body feeling? How is my heart feeling? How do I feel about my connection with God?

In what ways do I need support? How can I invite that support?

What do I want to pray about for next week? Who can I invite to pray with me and for me?

WEEK 5: FRIENDSHIPS

Time-Out: My Hopes, Prayers, and Goals for This Week

Libby looked up from tying her running shoes before cross-country practice. Melanie, another new girl, had just plopped down onto the grass nearby, stretching. Libby offered Melanie a smile, and Melanie smiled back.

Libby hesitated. She was still trying to find her place on the team, and just that morning she'd asked God to help her make a connection with someone at practice. Maybe Melanie's smile meant she was open to friendship.

Libby crammed a question past the tightness in her throat. "Hey, Melanie, youwannarunwithmetoday?" Her words rear-ended each other on the way out.

"Huh?" Melanie squinted at Libby.

Blushing, Libby made herself slow down. "Do you want to run with me today?"

"Oh." Melanie's smile turned plastic. "I was going to run with the varsity girls. Sorry."

"Oh, no worries, have a good run." Libby forced a too-big, no-I-don't-feel-totally-stupid grin.

Melanie stood up. "Maybe another time."

"Yep."

As Melanie jogged away, Libby ducked her head, trying to hide her embarrassment. She tried to give Melanie the benefit of the doubt. Maybe Melanie had already promised those girls she'd run with them. Maybe Libby just needed to ask earlier next time.

There never was a next time. Libby tried to strike up a few conversations with Melanie throughout the season, but Melanie usually rushed off to join the varsity girls as fast as she could. As the season went on, Libby began to understand the team dynamics more clearly: The varsity girls kept to themselves, showing little interest in running with or even speaking to anyone on JV. The two teams technically practiced together, but "together" really meant "in two separate groups that rarely interacted."

Libby loved running cross-country, but she hated the division on the team. She found herself struggling with resentment, along with insecurity and a sense of inferiority. *Why won't the varsity girls open their friend group up to the rest of us? Are we not worthy of friendship just because we don't run as fast as they do?*

She confessed her frustrations to her mom, the wisest person she knew. Mom thought for a minute, then said, "The best thing you can do is set a different example yourself."

Libby made a face. "Mom, no one is paying attention to my example—they're barely paying attention to me, period! I don't really have friends yet."

Mom gave a knowing grin. "But you will. That's the beautiful irony of being a Christian: When you give yourself away, you often end up finding what you need along the way. If you head into every practice looking to give—reaching out to quiet girls, pulling in the ones who seem left out and lonely—you'll plant seeds of change on your team. And before long, I bet you'll become friends with some of the girls you reach out to."

The next day as Libby walked to practice, she prayed a different prayer: "Lord, please show me someone else who is feeling alone. And please give me the courage to reach out."

As she reached the track where the team met to warm up and stretch, she saw a freshman sitting alone near the bleachers, fiddling with her laces.

Okay, God, here we go.

Libby walked over to the girl. "Hey! Mind if I stretch with you?"

The girl looked up with a shy smile, and Libby sat down.

PLANTING SEEDS OF CHANGE

I have called you friends, for everything that I learned from my Father I have made known to you.
John 15:15

WARM-UP

What makes you feel included on your team?

Libby's struggle to find friends on her team wasn't unusual. Cliquishness is a common problem on sports teams, but knowing it's a common problem doesn't make it any less miserable when you're the one stuck on the outside.

Have you ever thought about the fact that Jesus experienced rejection and exclusion too? He was misunderstood by the very people he'd come to save. The Bible tells us, "He came to his own people, and even they rejected him" (John 1:11 NLT). As Jesus's arrest drew near, he cried out, "Jerusalem, Jerusalem, you who kill the prophets and stone those sent to you, how often I have longed to gather your children together, as a hen gathers her chicks under her wings, and you were not willing" (Matthew 23:37). Can you hear the heartache in Jesus's words? He longed to love and lead his people, but they rejected his teaching and pushed him away. In the end, they killed him.

But Jesus didn't give up on friendship despite rejection. Throughout his ministry, Jesus offered the warmth of inclusion and the hope of salvation to people whom other religious leaders rejected. He spent time with tax collectors, sinners, poor people, sick people—all the lost and lonely, the ones the world overlooked and despised. He broke down gender and cultural barriers, inviting women and uneducated fishermen to participate in his ministry. He offered friendship to many people who didn't expect it—and some who didn't return it.

Knowing that Jesus understands the sting of rejection can take the edge off our pain when we feel excluded. Seeing that Jesus didn't give up on friendship can give us the determination to keep trying when we feel discouraged. Imitating Jesus's example of forgiveness can help us restore struggling friendships.

Like Jesus, we can model a different way—in the classroom and the locker room.

Like Jesus, we can reach out to the lost and lonely.

Like Jesus, we can plant seeds of change.

PRACTICE

Think about your teammates. Does anyone seem quiet or left out? How can you pull her in this week?

PLANTING SEEDS OF FRIENDSHIP

Remember this: Whoever sows sparingly will also reap sparingly, and whoever sows generously will also reap generously.
2 Corinthians 9:6

WARM-UP

What's your favorite thing to do with friends?

People talk a big game about friendships on athletic teams, don't they? "We're all besties! Close like sisters!" But the reality is, not everyone feels like that. Plenty of girls feel left out and lonely.

Maybe you're like Libby and you're new to a team, not sure how to break in. Or maybe you've been on a team for a while, but you feel stuck in a rut—same girls, same conversations, no meaningful connections. Maybe you had good friends last year, but this year's team is different and the vibe has changed. As lonely as those situations feel, you're not alone.

We talked yesterday about planting seeds of change; today, let's talk about planting seeds of friendship. In his second letter to the church in Corinth, Paul writes, "Remember this: Whoever sows sparingly will also reap sparingly, and whoever sows generously will also reap generously." In context, Paul is talking about the importance of financial generosity, but he is describing a life principle that applies in many areas, including friendship. Like a seed, friendship takes time to grow. And generosity makes a difference: The more seeds we plant, the more chances we have to see something bloom.

Remember the preschool science experiment where you planted a seed in a Styrofoam cup? You'd poke your fat white seed into dark, damp dirt, place the cup on a sunny windowsill, and wait. After a few days, a pale green shoot would curl out of the soil. If you want closer friendships on your team, try planting some seeds like you did back then.

What does it mean to plant a seed of friendship? It might mean...

- sending encouraging texts
- inviting someone to partner with you for warm-ups or drills
- asking a teammate to go out for smoothies after practice

Small acts like these might not feel like much, but they could blossom into real friendship as the season goes on. Not every seed you plant will grow, but *some will*. Keep planting, keep watering, and give God room to work.

PRACTICE

List two things you could do this week to plant seeds of friendship with your teammates:

1. ____________________

____

____

____

____

____

2. ____________________

____

____

____

____

____

WHAT'S YOUR GIFT?

In his grace, God has given us different gifts for doing certain things well. So if God has given you the ability to prophesy, speak out with as much faith as God has given you. If your gift is serving others, serve them well. If you are a teacher, teach well. If your gift is to encourage others, be encouraging. If it is giving, give generously. If God has given you leadership ability, take the responsibility seriously. And if you have a gift for showing kindness to others, do it gladly.
Romans 12:6–8 NLT

WARM-UP

How would you define your role on your team?

The soccer ball bounced free, and Andi couldn't resist—she chased after it. The minute she left her position, Coach's voice boomed: "Not your job, Andi! Get back!"

Reluctantly, Andi abandoned the chase and backpedaled to her place in front of the goal. Back to defense. Just in time too, because now the other team's strongest forward was breaking away with the ball, headed Andi's way. Andi got ready to engage.

You dedicate a lot of time to mastering your role on your team. Like Andi, maybe you're a defender, and it's your job to protect the goal. Maybe you play offense, and it's your job to put points on the board. Even in the more individual sports—like track and field, golf, tennis, swimming, or diving—every team member has a part to play.

But you have more than just an athletic role: you also have a spiritual one. Today's Scripture comes from Paul's letter to Christians in Rome, and he describes the way God assigns each person spiritual gifts—or spiritual strengths. Paul specifically lists serving, teaching, encouraging, giving, leading, and showing kindness. Certainly God calls us to exercise those gifts in our church families, but how might you also share your spiritual gifts with your team?

If you have the gift of serving, you probably excel at noticing what coaches and teammates need, then stepping in to meet those needs.

If you are a natural teacher, you can help less experienced players hone skills, learn drills, and master plays.

If you are an encourager, what a blessing you can be: pointing out teammates' victories and strengths, helping everyone stay positive.

If you are a leader, your team needs your strength. You set an example and set the pace. Your attitude and example can inspire your team to be their best.

As you lean into your athletic role on your team, don't forget to lean into your spiritual role too. You are spiritually gifted—why not share those gifts with your team?

PRACTICE

What spiritual gift(s) in Paul's list do you have? What's one way you can offer your spiritual gift(s) to your team this week?

RIVALS TO TEAMMATES

After David had finished talking with Saul, Jonathan became one in spirit with David, and he loved him as himself.
1 Samuel 18:1

WARM-UP

What's the most meaningful gift you've ever given or received from a friend?

David was a lowly shepherd boy who grew up protecting sheep in the wilderness; Jonathan was a prince who grew up fighting battles, training to become Israel's next king. Their paths never should have crossed, but God had a trick play up his sleeve. When Jonathan's father, Saul, failed as Israel's first king, God sent a prophet to appoint David as Israel's next king. Jonathan grew up expecting to be the next king of Israel, but God chose David instead. To put this in sports terms, an upstart freshman ousted the senior captain for the starting position.

When we meet Jonathan, we expect him to be jealous of David, hurt and angry that God is passing him over and handing his birthright to someone else. In fact, Jonathan's father *was* jealous and angry about David being the next to wear the crown—Saul tried to kill David multiple times. But Jonathan wasn't like that. He gave David his heart, his loyalty, and his friendship. And because Jonathan loved David as he loved himself, he gladly stepped aside to let his friend shine.

How differently their story could have gone! Theirs could have been a story about jealousy, vengeance, and hatred; instead, Jonathan's generous, humble heart made it a story about the most beautiful of friendships. Scripture tells us, "Jonathan made a covenant with David because he loved him as himself. Jonathan took off the robe he was wearing and gave it to David, along with his tunic, and even his sword, his bow and his belt" (1 Samuel 18:3-4). These symbolic gifts showed David—and the soldiers who witnessed the exchange—that Jonathan wasn't just David's friend; he also supported his success and leadership.

Sometimes in sports you are the one to lead and shine. You might be the up-and-coming player, the one everyone admires—or the established leader, the one who carries the team. Other times you may feel pushed aside by a teammate who takes your position. Maybe she's truly better than you, or maybe the coach favors her for reasons you don't understand. Whatever the reason, you have a choice to make just as Jonathan did: Will you view your teammate as a rival or a friend? Will you resent her success or cheer her on? Will you trust that God has a place for *both* of you in his story?

Jonathan chose the way of humility and friendship. What will you choose?

TAKE A KNEE

Father, thank you that you have plans for me, just as you have plans for my teammates and friends. Please help me to support others when they have success, and please protect my friendships even when we have different levels of success. I trust you with my sport and with my heart. In Jesus's name, amen.

WHAT SPIRITUAL FRIENDS DO

And Saul's son Jonathan went to David at Horesh and helped him find strength in God.
1 Samuel 23:16

WARM-UP

What qualities do you look for in friendships?

David and Jonathan's friendship shouldn't have worked, but it did. Why did their friendship work so well? Because they were young men who walked with God, trusted God, and invited his will to reign. Today's verse comes from a moment when David's life was at risk—he was hiding from Jonathan's jealous father, King Saul, who wanted to kill David—and Jonathan helped his friend draw strength from God.

When it comes to your friendships, maybe you value humor—you love to laugh and joke around. Maybe you seek friends with common interests—girls who like to do the same things you do. Or maybe you search for that mysterious thing we call "chemistry." It's hard to explain it, but we know it when we feel it: we just "click." David and Jonathan's example highlights a friendship quality far more important than humor, common interests, or chemistry: *spirituality*.

As you pray about finding or deepening friendships on your team this season, let David and Jonathan's example inspire your prayers. Ask God to lead you to spiritually minded friends who will help you find strength in God. Fun friends are . . . well, fun. But godly friends are good for the soul. Spiritual friends may not have all the same interests or even the same personality as you, but if they love God like you do, the friendship can be deep and meaningful:

Maybe you pray together before practice or games.

Maybe you swap encouraging Scriptures throughout the week.

Maybe you offer advice or support through difficult decisions.

As Libby experienced, friends—especially godly friends—can be tough to find. You may or may not have other Christians on your team this season. But even if you don't see options for spiritual friendships right now, that doesn't mean God isn't working to bring the relationships you need into your life. Just like Libby did, keep asking him to lead you to friends who love him as you do, knowing that in the meantime, God himself is your friend, and he'll keep you company all season long.

DRILL

How would you describe a spiritual friendship?

TAKING FRIENDSHIPS DEEPER

Because we loved you so much, we were delighted to share with you not only the gospel of God but our lives as well.
1 Thessalonians 2:8

WARM-UP

Which do you enjoy more in friendships: having deep talks or doing active things?

At this point in the season, maybe you've pushed through some of the intimidating please-let-me-in moments like Libby encountered, and you've begun to develop some friendships on your team. You feel comfortable, you're having fun, but . . . you'd like a little more out of the friendships. More depth. More spiritual encouragement. You'd like to develop a God-centered friendship like David and Jonathan's, but you're not sure how to get there, how to take things deeper.

Here we can learn from another Bible hero: the apostle Paul. Paul wasn't just a great missionary and theologian; he was also a devoted friend. The New Testament contains thirteen letters he wrote to churches and to individuals. In many of these letters, Paul sent greetings to specific friends he made on his missionary journeys. Although Paul was a highly educated Jewish man, he didn't restrict his relationships solely to other like-minded Jews; he befriended a wide variety of people from different nations, cultures, and religious backgrounds. While they had few outward traits in common, they shared a love for Jesus, and so they opened their hearts to one another in friendship.

Paul became close friends with new Christians in the city of Thessalonica, even though it's likely he had to leave quickly due to religious persecution (see Acts 17:1–10). Paul writes to his new friends in 1 Thessalonians with deep affection, saying, "Because we loved you so much, we were delighted to share with you not only the gospel of God but our lives as well."

How can their story help ours? Maybe there's another believer on your team, and you don't have much in common besides Jesus. From a worldly standpoint, the "friendship chemistry" isn't automatic, but you have Jesus as a starting place. So how can you draw closer? Like Paul and the Thessalonians, perhaps you can share more about your lives with one another. Maybe you ask about her family, her likes and dislikes, her sports history, her faith story. You don't have to jump into the deep end right away—simply sharing little things can build camaraderie, understanding, and trust.

Some bonds strengthen over time, but others, like Paul's friendship with the Thessalonians, grow quickly. The intensity of a sports season has a way of intensifying relational bonds: You share suffering and defeat, victory and joy. And those shared experiences can be meaningful and powerful.

Who knows? If you look for opportunities to share your life with potential friends on your team, God may surprise you with some deeper connections.

PRACTICE

Here are a few easy take-it-deeper questions that can help you get to know a new friend or deepen an existing friendship:

- How did you get into this sport? What's your favorite part about it?
- What's your family like?
- What else are you into besides sports?

STAY SALTY

Be wise in the way you act toward outsiders; make the most of every opportunity. Let your conversation be always full of grace, seasoned with salt, so that you may know how to answer everyone. Colossians 4:5–6

WARM-UP

Who would you like to get to know better on your team? Why?

Luz rolled an earbud between her fingertips; her favorite podcast was calling her name. She glanced around the crowded bus—most of her teammates were wearing earbuds or headphones, and the bus was oddly quiet considering thirty girls were crammed inside for a two-hour ride. But a little voice prodded her conscience: *This is the opportunity you've been looking for. Hadley's sitting across the aisle, and you've been praying for the chance to ask her how she's doing with her grandma being sick. Now's your chance. Just . . . be brave and say something.*

The nudge Luz felt inside was a godly one. Did you know the Bible encourages us to be salty? Not full-of-sass-and-bad-attitude salty—no, the Bible means something different. God wants our conversations to reach beyond bland and shallow topics; he wants us to flavor our words with faith and depth, just as Luz pondered doing with Hadley on the bus ride.

In today's passage, Paul encourages us to exercise wisdom in our relationships with non-believers, making the most of every opportunity to make a difference in others' lives. Sometimes I miss—or (if I'm being honest) totally avoid—opportunities to talk to people. Maybe I'm tired, maybe I'm grumpy, maybe my social battery is low. Do you relate? After a workout, you feel exhausted, ready to check out and have some "me time." On bus rides to away games, with nerves running high, you want to put earbuds in, disappear into your own mind and music, and amp yourself up for the game. We all have a million reasons to avoid conversations and stay inside our own heads, but as ambassadors for Christ, we're called to stay aware of the opportunities God gives us. To keep an eye out for chances to make connections, deepen friendships, and share our faith.

What does it mean to season a conversation with salt? It could mean mentioning God in a conversation. It could mean offering to pray for someone who's hurting or stressed. It could mean sharing a favorite Scripture with a teammate who's feeling discouraged or defeated. Sometimes simply sprinkling a few grains of spiritual salt into a conversation provides an opening that leads someone a step closer to God . . . or closer to you in friendship.

PRACTICE

It can be difficult to find time to talk—really talk—during practice and games. But if we pay attention, we can take advantage of opportunities to connect—between drills, during low-key warm-ups and cool-downs, on bus rides to away games. This week, look for an opportunity to make a connection with a teammate.

WEEKLY CHECK-IN

What went well this week? What was hard? Did I meet the goals I set for myself?

How is my body feeling? How is my heart feeling? How do I feel about my connection with God?

In what ways do I need support? How can I invite that support?

What do I want to pray about for next week? Who can I invite to pray with me and for me?

WEEK 6: RESILIENCE AND GRIT

Time-Out: My Hopes, Prayers, and Goals for This Week

Last Chance: Merlot's Story

Merlot stared up at the uneven bars, fighting to ignore the squirmy feeling inside. A little voice whispered, *Last chance to improve your score before the state gymnastics meet.* Her insides churned harder.

As she chalked her grips, she tuned out everything except the bar routine ahead. The buzz of the crowd and the cheers of her teammates faded to a dull hum.

She saluted the judges, took a deep breath, and swung into action.

First move, a kip pirouette—perfect. Next up, a free hip, a move she'd done hundreds of times in practice. She circled the low bar, swinging up into a handstand, and—her grips slipped off the bar, sending her flying, free-falling.

Sound returned to her ears as she fell—hundreds of horrified voices in the bleachers gasping, "Ooooh!"

She landed on her back, stunned and blinking up at the fluorescent lights shining down like mocking stars.

The gym was silent.

For two seconds—which felt like two years—Merlot's body lay still as her brain scanned for injury. She wiggled her fingers, her toes, her neck. Eased up to a seated position, still assessing. Cataloguing pain. A mild ache in her shoulder—manageable. A sting in her palm—a new rip. Not fun, but she was used to rips.

Time sped back up as her coach rushed forward, a worried question in his eyes: *Are you okay?* She waved him away. "I'm good," she called.

Relief rushed across his face, then he tapped his watch. "Thirty seconds to remount."

Merlot's brain kick-started, thoughts now flying. If she didn't resume her routine within thirty seconds, she'd be disqualified. She sprang to her feet and rushed to the chalk bucket.

As she re-chalked her grips, her hands trembled—from adrenaline or fear? Probably both.

She glanced back up at the bars. Her heart kicked fast in her chest, pounding out objections: *Don't-do-this-don't-do-this.*

Clouds of chalk puffed around her face; panicked thoughts swirled inside her head. *What if it happens again? What if I come off the high bar this time?*

It was a one-time fluke, she coached herself, trying to push back the fear. *You've done this routine safely a million times.*

Ten seconds left.

She stepped back up to the apparatus, heart thumping, shoulder throbbing, hand burning. The crowd cheered as she stared down the bars.

I can do this. Stop thinking, just go. Time's up, go now!

Merlot remounted, swung into her free hip, hit the handstand, and finished the move safely. *Yes!*

Next a squat-on, a leap to the high bar, and then she swung into two giants, huge looping circles around the high bar. *Grips, don't fail me now.*

Her mind shouted a reminder—*Toes!*—and she pulled her toes in so they wouldn't hit the low bar. Clear. One more giant, then she released the high bar for a layout dismount.

The world went topsy-turvy as she flipped.

She stuck the landing, feet planted, arms outstretched, smile huge.

She saluted the judges, then the crowd, to a roar of applause.

As she ran off the mat, she gave a thousand high fives.

Her score wouldn't be anywhere near what she'd hoped for, but Merlot felt proud of this routine. Maybe prouder than any routine she'd done all season. She'd fought back from a fall. Fought back from fear.

"How do you feel?" Coach asked.

"Great." Merlot smiled. "This will be the best bad score I've ever gotten."

"If they gave medals for grit," her coach said, "you'd get the gold."

I WON'T STAY DOWN

But we have this treasure in jars of clay to show that this all-surpassing power is from God and not from us. We are hard pressed on every side, but not crushed; perplexed, but not in despair; persecuted, but not abandoned; struck down, but not destroyed. We always carry around in our body the death of Jesus, so that the life of Jesus may also be revealed in our body.
2 Corinthians 4:7–10

WARM-UP

What Scripture or truth helps you trust God when life is difficult?

The apostle Paul wrote 2 Corinthians during a profoundly difficult time in his ministry. The stakes for Paul were much higher than getting a high score in a meet or winning a championship—Paul and his companions were seeking to spread the good news of Jesus Christ, and they were risking their lives to do it. Sometimes they were arrested, sometimes beaten, sometimes nearly killed.

Paul described their frail human bodies as jars of clay, easily broken—but these fragile jars contained eternal treasure, "all-surpassing power." God's power.

Knowing he could turn to God for strength, Paul cultivated an attitude of resilience. An attitude that helped him survive heartache, disappointment, and trial. An attitude that helped him get up every time he got knocked down. Paul wrote, "We are hard pressed . . . but not crushed; perplexed, but not in despair; persecuted, but not abandoned; struck down, but not destroyed."

Paul acknowledged the hard things, but he refused to let those things defeat him. He trusted that God's power could sustain him through every difficulty.

Paul knew that persecution didn't mean God had abandoned him.

And every time life knocked Paul down, he got up again.

We can learn from Paul's resilience when life, or sports, aren't going the way we'd hoped. When we find ourselves lying flat on our backs, wondering how we got there, God can help us get back on our feet. When we're staring up at our next challenge, facing what-if-I-fall-again fears, his presence gives us courage to try again. In such moments, we can imitate Paul's resilience—and Merlot's—with empowering thoughts like:

- *I'm under pressure, but I'm not giving up. I can depend on God's power to keep me going.*
- *I don't understand why my season is going this way, but I'm not letting discouragement overwhelm me.*
- *I may have fallen, but I refuse to stay down. With God's help, I will get up and keep fighting.*

PRACTICE

Write a sentence or two describing a resilient thought you can focus on through whatever challenge you're currently facing.

THE PAYOFF OF PERSEVERANCE

So do not throw away your confidence; it will be richly rewarded. You need to persevere so that when you have done the will of God, you will receive what he has promised. For, "In just a little while, he who is coming will come and will not delay."
Hebrews 10:35–37

WARM-UP

How have you already shown perseverance in your faith or your sport this season?

"Why aren't my times getting faster? Why do I keep collapsing at the finish line?" I hoped my coach didn't hear the way my voice was wobbling. "I trained like crazy all summer, but . . ." I didn't need to finish. We both knew the end of the sentence: *I'm not having the senior season I was supposed to have. The season I trained to have.*

Coach said some nice things, but I didn't feel better. I felt trapped. Frustrated. Confused. Betrayed by my own body.

We're talking this week about resilience and grit. Hebrews 10 is a powerful read, all about persevering in faith, remaining confident that on the other side of our hardships, God has an eternal reward in store.

Sports are good practice for our faith. Maybe you've experienced a plateau, similar to that awful "stuck" feeling I had my senior year. And you've probably experienced some moments like Merlot's fall, times when you had to dust yourself off and try again despite failure or fear. Tough sports situations force us to push through hard days, find positivity after disappointments, and dig deep for courage. We need similar qualities in our faith walk. Being a Christian isn't always easy—sometimes it's unpopular and even painful. You may experience difficult moments because of your faith, moments when following Jesus calls you to stand apart or stand alone.

When friends pass around an inappropriate video, you might need to look away and risk being called a prude.

When the locker room talk turns cruel, you might have to leave the conversation or stand up for the underdog.

In moments like these, you might wish following Jesus were easier. You might be tempted to compromise, to blend in. You might wish being a Christian made you cool instead of different. These are times to remember the promise in Hebrews: "Do not throw away your confidence; it will be richly rewarded. You need to persevere so that when you have done the will of God, you will receive what he has promised."

Our confidence isn't in people's opinions—our confidence is in God. That's a confidence worth keeping, worth the effort to persevere. When we keep living and loving like Jesus, we fulfill God's will. And when we fulfill God's will, we receive his promises.

DRILL

How can you tell you are putting your confidence in God?

TOUGH TIMES DON'T HAVE TO BE WASTED TIME

It was not you who sent me here, but God.
Genesis 45:8

WARM-UP

When have you seen a "bad" situation turn into something good?

Unfairness is miserable. Maybe you feel stuck on a team where you're unappreciated. Maybe you feel cheated out of a position you deserve. Or maybe, like Merlot, you've experienced a fluke misfortune that set you back.

Sometimes we can speak up and fight for change, but other times we can't do much. We feel powerless, trapped. We find ourselves wrestling with thorny, "it's not supposed to be this way" realities:

- Coaches are supposed to be fair, but sometimes they aren't.
- Teammates are supposed to be selfless, but sometimes they aren't.
- Hard work is supposed to pay off, but sometimes it doesn't.

When we're stuck in an unfair situation, we have choices to make about how we think and act. Choices about who we become during a painful time. Today let's learn from an Israelite teenager whose life didn't go the way it was "supposed" to go. At seventeen, Joseph was sold into slavery by his jealous brothers. (Talk about unfair!) He lived as a slave and a prisoner for years. But he kept working hard, trusting God, and persevering. In the end—and by "the end" we mean "after many long, miserable years"—God honored Joseph's integrity and faith, raising him to a position of power and enabling him to save many lives, including those of his family.

After Joseph was reunited with his brothers, he forgave them, saying, "It was not you who sent me here, but God. . . . You intended to harm me, but God intended it for good to accomplish what is now being done, the saving of many lives" (Genesis 45:8, 50:20).

Joseph's story is a powerful example of God bringing good out of a terrible situation. As Romans 8:28 says, "In all things God works for the good of those who love him." All things are not good, but God can work *through* all things (even unfair things) to bring about good.

How might God bring about good through unfair sports situations? He helps us cultivate character traits we can't develop when life is easy—traits like perseverance, humility, and patience. He uses tough circumstances to deepen our prayer life as we rely on him. He reminds us we can shine a light for Jesus by facing difficulties with courage and positivity.

Joseph's story inspires us to persevere when life isn't going our way. It also reminds us that tough times don't have to be wasted time. No one can stop us from working hard, growing stronger, and getting better. Tough times aren't fun, but they *are* opportunities. When unfairness strikes, we can strike back by refusing to waste a chance to grow.

DRILL

Recall a time when you saw God working behind the scenes in your life. How does that memory strengthen your trust in God?

____

____

____

____

____

____

____

THE MIDSEASON SLUMP

Not that I have already obtained all this, or have already arrived at my goal, but I press on to take hold of that for which Christ Jesus took hold of me. Brothers and sisters, I do not consider myself yet to have taken hold of it. But one thing I do: Forgetting what is behind and straining toward what is ahead, I press on toward the goal to win the prize for which God has called me heavenward in Christ Jesus.
Philippians 3:12–14

WARM-UP

What's hard about the middle of the season?

"Are you excited for tonight's game?"

Alanna flashed her dad a forced grin. "Yeah, sure."

Dad pegged Alanna with a peering-deep-into-her-soul look that made her squirm. "'Yeah, sure?'" he asked, mimicking her inflection. "What's wrong?"

Alanna shrugged. "I just don't feel hype, you know? We're midway through the season, and I just feel . . . *meh*. Tired and uninspired. But I know if I don't pull it together, Coach will pull me out—and then I won't feel *meh*—I'll feel *mad*."

The midseason slump can be very real. As exhaustion runs high, excitement runs low. Once the thrill of a new season wears off, the days may become a grind. Same drills, same rants—er, speeches—from coaches; same girls, same drama. It's easy to become complacent, drifting through on autopilot. If we don't reassume the controls, that complacency can set us up for sloppy play or surprise defeats.

Complacency can be a dangerous mindset in our spiritual lives too. When we consistently neglect spiritual practices like prayer, Bible study, and worship, we lose inspiration. And when we drift through our walk with God without inspiration, we gradually grow dull. We may engage in "sloppy play" by setting a poor example in our speech or lifestyle. We may fall prey to surprise defeats—temptations that draw us into sin—because we're not paying attention.

Let's revisit a mindset that kept the apostle Paul spiritually motivated: "Not that I have already obtained all this, or have already arrived at my goal, but I press on to take hold of that for which Christ Jesus took hold of me" (Philippians 3:12).

Paul kept laser-focused on his long-term goal: becoming like Christ. And becoming like Jesus is a lifelong challenge because Jesus was perfect. Just as we never run a perfect race or perform a perfect routine, we will never "arrive" at the goal of becoming like our perfect Savior—we always have room to grow. Knowing this, Paul was committed to a lifetime of personal growth. A lifetime of passionate discipleship. How did he stay motivated? By keeping his eyes on the "prize" of becoming more and more like Jesus.

Where do you need motivation right now? If you've been feeling dull in your walk with God, perhaps you can rekindle inspiration by reconnecting in prayer. If you've been feeling *meh* about your season like Alanna was, perhaps you can renew motivation by making some second-half-of-the-season goals. Like Paul, when we keep our eyes on the prize of growth, we experience the excitement of continued progress. We turn *meh* into motivation, and a midseason slump into a midseason surge.

DRILL

Choose the question that best applies to your season so far, then write your response in the space provided.

- If things are going well so far, how can you build off that exciting momentum?
- If things aren't going the way you'd hoped, how can you dig deep to keep growing as an athlete and teammate?

____

____

____

SWEAT THE SMALL STUFF

If you are faithful in little things, you will be faithful in large ones.
Luke 16:10 NLT

WARM-UP

What's your favorite drill or exercise? How does it make a difference in your training?

Eighteen . . . nineteen . . . twenty. Arms trembling, Cecily paused. She was supposed to do ten more push-ups, but . . . She glanced up. Coach wasn't looking. *Twenty push-ups is close enough to thirty. What Coach doesn't know can't hurt her.*

Cecily stood up, then paused. Her teammate Abigail was still going, grinding out numbers between her teeth. "Twenty-nine . . . argh . . . thirty." Abigail collapsed face-down onto the grass, then rolled over with a big, *I-did-it* grin.

"Way to work," Cecily said, feeling a twinge of guilt-tipped admiration as she reached a hand down to help her friend up.

"I'm so slow," Abigail said. "Everyone else hits thirty way faster than me."

Cecily bit her lip. "Honestly? No one else is doing all thirty."

"Really?" Abigail's eyes went wide.

Cecily gave her a friendly punch in the arm. "Now we know why your throwing arm is the strongest on the team. We all need to be more like you."

Abigail grinned. "I guess every push-up helps."

In Luke 16, Jesus told a parable about a servant who put his master's money to good use. Jesus noted, "If you are faithful in little things, you will be faithful in large ones." Jesus was saying that when we give our best effort in small responsibilities, we prepare ourselves to handle—and perhaps we earn the opportunity to handle—bigger ones.

Small daily decisions are places where we build—and reveal—our character. In sports, small daily drills are where we build habits, skills, and conditioning. How we handle those small decisions is up to us, because honestly? It's easy to cut corners if we want to. Easy to make workouts a little shorter when Coach isn't looking. Ten push-ups might not make much difference today, but over time, all that conditioning adds up.

When I was a kid, my dad had a saying: "Who you are when you're alone is who you really are." The things we do (and don't do) when no one is watching define our true character. The things we do (and don't do) when no one is holding us accountable determine the kind of person we will become.

In Luke 16:11, Jesus went on to ask, "And if you are untrustworthy about worldly wealth, who will trust you with the true riches of heaven?" Worldly tasks like homework, chores, and Coach's on-your-own conditioning runs are practice ground for life's bigger responsibilities: college life, a serious dating relationship, a career, a family.

It turns out that training for sports is training for life, but in disguise. Sometimes, it's smart to sweat the small stuff, because small stuff can make a big difference.

TAKE A KNEE

Dear Father, thank you for caring about the small details of my life. Please give me the character and consistency I need to work hard in the small things. I want to honor you by having integrity in all I do. In Jesus's name, amen.

BUT GOD KNOWS

Whatever you do, work at it with all your heart, as working for the Lord, not for human masters, since you know that you will receive an inheritance from the Lord as a reward. It is the Lord Christ you are serving.
Colossians 3:23–24

WARM-UP

What stat do you *wish* they kept in your sport?

Jazz stared at her phone, feeling her heart kick faster. "These stats can't be for real! I played way better than this!"

Mom peered over her shoulder. "Well—numbers aren't everything."

"They kind of are, though," Jazz insisted. "People care about stats, and these numbers are embarrassing." Jazz struggled to find the right words. "With stats like these, no one will know I played well. Maybe I shouldn't care, but . . ." She finished the sentence in her mind: *I do care. I really, really care.*

Mom was quiet for a moment. "Someone else knows you played well."

"Who?"

"God."

Sometimes stats get it wrong. Or they get it right, but they don't tell the whole story. Stats can't record your effort, your heart, your growth. They don't capture the way you led your team on the field, or encouraged other runners on back trails when they were struggling, or gave a friend a pep talk before her heat.

There's no Got Back Up Every Time She Fell stat, or Did Extra Push-Ups and Sprints at Home stat, or Never Missed a Six A.M. Summer Workout Even When She Wanted to Sleep In stat. Nobody records those things. Even coaches don't always notice those things.

And stats (or the lack thereof) aren't the only issue. Sometimes you simply feel overlooked. No one seems to notice the selfless leadership you quietly contribute behind the scenes. No one sees your internal victory over fear every time you perform a scary stunt. Or no one remembers your epic, game-saving play because someone else had an even more epic, game-saving play. Those moments test our hearts, our humility, and our motivation: *Why* do we sacrifice and give our all if no one even sees it?

Paul gives us an answer: "Whatever you do, work at it with all your heart, as working for the Lord, not for human masters, since you know that you will receive an inheritance from the Lord as a reward. It is the Lord Christ you are serving." Paul's words were originally meant for the Christians in Colossae who worked as domestic servants or were enslaved—people who were all too familiar with working hard for little to no praise or acknowledgment. Paul invited them to consider an empowering and redemptive perspective: to offer their effort to Jesus as a holy offering. You and I can apply a similar attitude when we feel unseen and unappreciated in a sport. You're not working for your coach, or for stats, or to impress anyone. You're working hard to honor God—and God sees and knows all you do.

When you drag yourself out of your warm bed and tiptoe out of your still-sleeping house to head to a predawn practice, God knows. When your great game is overshadowed by someone else's, God knows. When your stats don't tell the full story, God knows. When you pour out your heart, *his* heart swells with pride. And that's a reward worth fighting for.

DRILL

What work are you proudest of?

____

____

____

____

MOTIVATION FOR THE BY-YOURSELF DAYS

Where can I go from your Spirit? Where can I flee from your presence? If I go up to the heavens, you are there; if I make my bed in the depths, you are there. If I rise on the wings of the dawn, if I settle on the far side of the sea, even there your hand will guide me, your right hand will hold me fast.
Psalm 139:7–10

WARM-UP

Do you prefer to work out alone or in a group?

Accountability can be a good thing, a needed thing—we all train a little harder when we feel our teammates' or coaches' eyes on us. We experience powerful motivation and the joy of camaraderie when we encourage one another to go a little faster, push a little harder. But every athlete has times when she has to motivate herself all by herself. She has to get up early. Work out alone in the dark. Train in the offseason. Do the same old drill alone in the backyard for the millionty-billionth time.

Psalm 139 is a gorgeous psalm celebrating God's presence and activity in our lives. No matter where we go, God's loving presence goes with us. He'll meet us in the depths of discouragement and the silence of loneliness—he's not scared away by intense feelings. He'll meet us on the floor after a fall, whispering comfort to our fears.

God is always awake and never too busy. He never has a schedule conflict. He's always available, always there. That means when you show up for those all-by-yourself training times, you're not actually alone. God's keeping you company, and you can chat with him in prayer all throughout your workout. You can also stay connected as you train by playing worship music or listening to his Word.

If you feel most motivated when someone spurs you on, why not imagine God's voice saying, "One more rep, I know you've got it in you." You can envision him cheering you on through that last lap, that scary routine, that difficult drill.

God is with you and for you. Before dawn and after midnight. Off the field and on the field. In sports and in life.

PRACTICE

How can you stay more aware of God's presence throughout your day?

WEEKLY CHECK-IN

What went well this week? What was hard? Did I meet the goals I set for myself?

How is my body feeling? How is my heart feeling? How do I feel about my connection with God?

In what ways do I need support? How can I invite that support?

What do I want to pray about for next week? Who can I invite to pray with me and for me?

WEEK 7: LEADERSHIP

Time-Out: My Hopes, Prayers, and Goals for This Week

Ready or Not: Annabelle's Story

The crowded locker room was a tornado of activity. Annabelle picked her way to her locker across an obstacle course of cleats, water bottles, goggles, and lacrosse sticks. She put on her shooting shirt, adrenaline humming through her veins, as if her entire body were shouting, *We've been training all year for this! First game, let's go!* This was her favorite feeling in the whole world—well, her favorite feeling besides winning a game and celebrating with teammates.

She checked the clock—fifteen minutes till they had to be on the field for warm-ups. Any minute now she'd hear Sara's voice calling out over the hubbub, "Anybody who wants to pray before the game, follow me!"

And then she remembered: *Sara graduated. She's not here to organize the prayer.*

Annabelle scanned the locker room, wondering who would take charge of the prayer this year. As time ticked by, realization dawned: *No one is going to call for prayer without Sara here.*

Annabelle started to reach for her gear and head out to the field early, but then she paused. She really wanted to pray before this game. *Needed* to pray before this game. She needed to bring her worries and hopes and fears to God, to ask him for protection and guidance and the comfort of his presence. She felt a nudge inside. *If you want to bring an element of faith to this team, you're going to have to do it yourself. It's time to step up. Ready or not, it's time to lead.*

Annabelle's nerves kicked up a notch as her eyes darted around the locker room. A rap song had begun blasting from a portable speaker. Her teammates were dancing and scream-singing along, pumping themselves up. Would anyone else even want to pause to pray? What if Annabelle stepped up to lead, but no one followed?

Only one way to find out. She took a deep breath and raised her voice loud enough to be heard over the booming bass beat.

"Whoever wants to pray before the game, we're meeting in the back of the showers!"

A few girls glanced her way but went right back to dancing and rapping.

Pretending a confidence she didn't feel, Annabelle marched back to the showers, giving her hips a little jiggle in time with the beat, as if to say, *Yeah, I love Jesus, and I love to pray—but I can get hyped too.*

For two excruciating minutes, she stood alone beside the showers. Counting tiles. Noticing the mildew. Feeling more alone with every passing second.

But three minutes later, she heard the sound of giggles and footsteps. Two girls walked back to join her. Another teammate quickly followed.

Annabelle grinned at them. "All right, girls, let's pray."

TIME TO LEAD

Don't let anyone look down on you because you are young, but set an example for the believers in speech, in conduct, in love, in faith and in purity.
1 Timothy 4:12

WARM-UP

What excites you about the idea of setting an example for Jesus? What intimidates you?

The apostle Paul had a young disciple named Timothy. The New Testament contains two letters Paul wrote to Timothy, encouraging and equipping him for ministry. Timothy was young, perhaps younger than many of the people he was leading, and it seems he sometimes struggled to lead with confidence. Paul encouraged Timothy to embrace his God-given leadership role by saying, "Don't let anyone look down on you because you are young, but set an example for the believers in speech, in conduct, in love, in faith and in purity."

Timothy's age and inexperience didn't matter to God—because God had work he needed Timothy to do. In the same way, God has work he needs you to do at home, at school, at church, and on your team.

Paul urged Timothy to lead by example. To lead the way in his speech, conduct, love, faith, and in the purity of his life. Paul's words can be a great reminder for us too: God is relying on us to set an example for the people around us—including teammates.

That may sound inspiring on paper, but it can be intimidating to do in real life. As Timothy discovered in his church, and Annabelle learned in the locker room, sometimes we have to step up and lead before we feel ready to do it.

Like Annabelle, you might wish an older Christian were around to make the first move—but either you don't have a mature Christian on your team, or she's there but she's not bold enough to take the lead. That means it's up to you.

What are some ways you might need to lead?

Maybe you're like Annabelle, and you want to pray with your teammates. How can you initiate prayer, setting an example with your own faith?

Or maybe you wish your team came to practice with more intensity and focus. How can you encourage that through your own conduct?

You might wish the culture on your team were different—less gossipy, more encouraging. How can you help create an inclusive, positive atmosphere?

Sometimes we share our faith with our words; other times we shine a light through our example, including our actions and our attitudes.

How is God calling you to lead today?

PRACTICE

Paul encouraged Timothy to set an example in five areas: in his speech, behavior, love, faith, and in the purity of his life. Which of those five areas is your greatest strength?

AMBASSADORS

And he has committed to us the message of reconciliation. We are therefore Christ's ambassadors, as though God were making his appeal through us. We implore you on Christ's behalf: Be reconciled to God.
2 Corinthians 5:19–20

WARM-UP

When you think of someone who represents Jesus well, who do you picture, and why?

"Everybody circle up! All eyes on me!"

Under her visor, Coach's eyes took on their most serious squint. "Congrats on making the team. Now, you are no longer an individual; you are part of this team. That means everything you do represents the rest of your teammates—and it represents *me*."

She circled slowly, drilling laser eyes into each girl as she spoke. "On the sidelines, on the bus, in your classes—*everywhere you go*—you represent all of us. So when you leave here, I expect you to watch what you say and how you act. Now get out there and make us proud."

You've probably heard some version of that speech a hundred times (and you'll likely hear it a hundred more). But as a Christian athlete, you have an even bigger responsibility than simply representing your team: You also represent Jesus. In a letter to the Corinthian church, Paul shared his conviction that he and his ministry companions were Christ's ambassadors, or representatives. You and I can adopt that same perspective: Jesus himself isn't going to put on a uniform and join your team, but he's still there. Jesus is part of your team because *you* are on your team. He has sent you to represent him—to be his ambassador.

What does it mean to be an ambassador for Christ on an athletic team? It means showing up to practice, workouts, and competitions with a powerful purpose: to honor Jesus in all you do and say. Being an ambassador for Christ could mean . . .

- representing Jesus's wholehearted spirit by leading the way in effort and positivity—even on tough days when nothing's going right
- reflecting Jesus's compassion by encouraging and including team members who sometimes get overlooked
- modeling Jesus's self-control by staying calm when refs make questionable calls or opponents are obnoxious
- inviting Jesus's influence by offering to lead your team in prayer, like Annabelle did

Being appointed an ambassador is an honor. It's a position of trust and leadership: Jesus has put his reputation in our hands. As we head out to practice or competition, Jesus isn't squinting laser eyes at us from under a visor, but he still might say, "You're representing me today. Now get out there and make me proud!"

TAKE A KNEE

Lord, thank you for the privilege of representing you. Please strengthen me and give me wisdom as I strive to exemplify your ways today. In Jesus's name, amen.

UPSIDE-DOWN LEADERSHIP

Whoever wants to be a leader among you must be your servant, and whoever wants to be first among you must become your slave. For even the Son of Man came not to be served but to serve others and to give his life as a ransom for many.
Matthew 20:26–28 NLT

WARM-UP

Who do you admire as a leader? Why does their example inspire you?

Imagine one of your teammates marching up to your coach and announcing, "Coach, I'm clearly the best player here, so I want you to start me next game. And while you're at it, make me captain." The rest of the team would be like, "Excuse me, why do you think you're better than the rest of us?"

That's basically what happened with Jesus's disciples in Matthew 20. Two of the Twelve, James and John, asked Jesus to give them positions of power and honor. When the other ten guys caught wind of this, they were furious. Jesus's team started falling apart, so like a good coach, he pulled them together for a talk about what leadership is—and what it isn't.

You've probably experienced power struggles like this in sports; many teams have complex leadership dynamics. For one thing, the very qualities that make some athletes successful can also make them hard to work with. Strengths can *also* be weaknesses. For example, a fierce competitive drive is an asset . . . until it drives a player to become selfish, hogging the ball and the attention. Or what about when confidence—usually a good thing—twists into something not so good, like pride? And though strong leadership is essential to a team's success, what happens when *everyone* wants to be the leader? (I'll give you one word: *drama*.)

As a Christian and a strong woman, I've sometimes felt unsure about how to lead. *Is it okay to be assertive and take charge, or is that prideful? Does demonstrating humility mean I should run away from all compliments and attention?* To answer those questions, let's consider this: Jesus didn't rebuke James, John, or any of the Twelve for having ambition. He didn't say, "What's wrong with you guys? Your desire to lead means you are prideful and selfish." Jesus didn't criticize their ambition—he just redirected it.

Jesus went on to turn the worldly definition of leadership upside-down. He said, "The rulers in this world lord it over their people . . . But among you it will be different" (vv. 25–26 NLT). While worldly leaders expect special favors and treatment, Christlike leaders are humble and happy to give. Like Annabelle, they lead and perform acts of service without seeking thanks or praise. While worldly leaders take all the attention and accolades for themselves, Christlike leaders accept praise with grace, but they also honor others. Their generous spirit makes room for everyone on the team to excel and be celebrated.

If you have ambitions to lead, that's a good thing! Don't squash your leadership ability or hesitate to initiate—leadership is a spiritual gift from God. He invites us to lead as Jesus did: selflessly, humbly, generously. When we lead like that, we bring him glory.

PRACTICE

What's one way you can exercise Christlike leadership on your team this week?

____

____

____

____

LEAD FROM THE BENCH

But the LORD said to Samuel, "Do not consider his appearance or his height, for I have rejected him. The LORD does not look at the things people look at. People look at the outward appearance, but the LORD looks at the heart."
1 Samuel 16:7

WARM-UP

What leadership quality do you want to develop?

God was looking for a new king to lead his people. The first king, Saul, had looked the part: tall, handsome, intimidating. If Saul had been an athlete, he would have been the player with the most impressive physique. But Saul turned out to be a terrible leader.

So God sent the prophet Samuel to appoint a new king, and this time God chose David, a shepherd boy. As the youngest son in a large family, David was overlooked and taken for granted at home (see 1 Samuel 16:1–13). David wasn't as outwardly impressive as Saul, but he had a quality Saul lacked: a godly heart. When God looks for leaders, he doesn't prioritize appearance, accomplishments, or athleticism—he prioritizes *heart*.

It's easy to assume that the best athletes make the best leaders. But that's not always true, is it? Leadership isn't about skills, stats, or physique—it's about character. Yesterday we talked about how Jesus's upside-down definition of leadership emphasizes an attitude of service and humility. In other words, leadership is about heart. Leading with heart in your sport might mean . . .

- setting an example in your work ethic, resilience, and overall attitude
- encouraging players who lack confidence
- helping with unglamorous, behind-the-scenes tasks without expecting thanks or praise
- speaking up to initiate prayer or bringing a godly perspective to conversations

These actions don't require athletic skill or experience—they require a godly attitude. That means you don't have to be a senior, star player, or stat leader to make a difference on your team. You don't have to be named captain. You can lead from right where you are, even if it's on the bench.

DRILL

How can you help your team from behind the scenes?

CONFIDENT OR COCKY?

"The LORD who rescued me from the paw of the lion and the paw of the bear will rescue me from the hand of this Philistine."
1 Samuel 17:37

WARM-UP

In what skill do you feel most confident?

When King Saul failed as a king, God chose an unknown shepherd boy named David to be Israel's future leader. As David's story plays out, we learn more about his heart and why God picked him.

When we first meet David, the Israelites are at war with the Philistines, and they are being mocked by a supersoldier named Goliath. Every day, Goliath issued a public challenge: *Find one Israelite brave enough to fight me. Winner takes all—the champion wins the war for his nation.* For forty days, Goliath made his stand, insulting the armies of God. For forty days, the Israelites cowered in fear.

David showed up to deliver supplies to his older brothers, who were soldiers in Saul's army. When David heard Goliath's insults, he was livid. Like Annabelle, he stepped up when no one else would. Annabelle offered to pray; David offered to take on the giant: "Let no one lose heart on account of this Philistine; your servant will go and fight him."

David's boldness is staggering: He was a gangly teenage boy, not a soldier. But his next words reveal the source of his confidence. He began by listing his qualifications—his stats, if you will: "When a lion or a bear came and carried off a sheep from the flock, I went after it, struck it and rescued the sheep from its mouth. When it turned on me, I seized it by its hair, struck it and killed it" (vv. 34-35). David isn't bragging, just stating the facts: *I've got monster-slaying experience. I can do this.*

David quickly turned the attention away from himself, giving God credit for his past victories: "The LORD who rescued me from the paw of the lion and the paw of the bear will rescue me from the hand of this Philistine." Sure, David had practiced many hours with his slingshot. Yes, he had cultivated his skills and athleticism. But he knew his victories had come from the Lord—and would always come from the Lord.

David's example shows us that it's not wrong to be confident in our skills, bold in our pursuits, and hopeful of success. Sometimes, just as Israel needed David to lead, your team will need you to step up boldly: *Put me in, Coach. I'll take the shot. I'll anchor the relay.*

If you're concerned about coming across as cocky, remember the difference: A cocky player draws attention to herself, while a confident player points the spotlight back to God. She knows where her skills, talents, opportunities, and victories come from. She gives God glory—and God gives her confidence.

PRACTICE

How can you give God credit for your victories?

WHEN YOU'RE NOT A NATURAL LEADER

And who knows but that you have come to your royal position for such a time as this?
Esther 4:14

WARM-UP

Which do you prefer: leadership positions or supporting roles?

So far this week we've gotten to know some famous leaders in the Bible, including James, John, David, Timothy, and Paul. Today we'll learn from a woman named Esther, who became the queen of Persia.

It's possible that Esther didn't want to be queen. As an unmarried Jewish woman, she was "invited" to participate in a nationwide search for a new wife for the king of Persia. (I suspect this invitation only offered one RSVP choice: *Of course, what an honor.*)

We don't know much about Esther's personality, but despite the fact that she won the king's favor and became queen, she doesn't come across as a natural leader. She seems pleasant and poised, but not especially powerful. She didn't rock the boat, just did as she was told.

But God had bigger plans for Esther than living as a pampered royal. A spiteful man named Haman convinced King Xerxes—who didn't know his new wife was Jewish—to have all the Jews in Persia killed. And just like that, Esther had to do something. She alone had the power to rescue her people because she alone had the ear of the king. It was time to lead. Time to step up, speak up, and save the day.

Perhaps you relate to Esther: You prefer to keep your head down, work hard, and stay out of drama. You don't have to be in charge to be happy—you understand the value of supporting roles. You're confident in your contributions to your team, and you don't need anyone to shout your name from the rooftops. (Honestly, all that shouting is kind of embarrassing.)

But then you get forced into a position of leadership: A starter gets hurt, and Coach says, "I need you." A senior graduates, and if you don't lead your team in prayer, no one else will. Like Esther thousands of years ago, and Annabelle not so long ago, you have a decision to make.

At first, Esther was terrified and tried to get out of leading. But her cousin Mordecai helped her to see God's hand at work, saying, "Who knows but that you have come to your royal position for such a time as this?"

For such a time as this.

Those are powerful words. Perhaps they apply to your life this season: God chose you to be on this team, with this coach, with these players, right now. God made you *you*, with your personality, character, and athletic skills. If you're being called to lead, maybe Esther's story can help you find the courage to step up, speak up, and save the day. God has you where you are . . . for such a time as this.

TAKE A KNEE

Father, thank you for paying attention to my life. Please give me the courage to fulfill your purposes for me and to play whatever role my team needs me to play. In Jesus's name, amen.

COMMON GROUND

Yes, I try to find common ground with everyone, doing everything I can to save some. I do everything to spread the Good News and share in its blessings.
1 Corinthians 9:22–23 NLT

WARM-UP

What's your favorite way to connect with new people? (Music? Movies? Food? Sports? Faith?)

Do you ever feel like the oddball on your team, the one who doesn't get the dirty jokes or follow all the gossip? Feeling different isn't necessarily a bad thing—it can mean you're living Jesus's way in a world that doesn't. But at the same time, you know Jesus calls you be a light and to lead others toward him, and that means finding points of connection.

The apostle Paul faced the same challenge. Paul had been raised as a devout, highly educated Jew, but then he met Jesus, and Jesus appointed him to be the "apostle to the Gentiles" (Romans 11:13; see also Acts 22:17–21). Paul spent years traveling to different nations, spreading the gospel. He left Israel and journeyed throughout Asia Minor, the Mediterranean, and Europe. Most of the people Paul ministered to were not Jewish like he was. And yet Paul was an effective preacher, bringing people from many cultures and religious backgrounds to faith in Christ.

In his first letter to the church in Corinth, Paul explained his strategy: "I try to find common ground with everyone, doing everything I can to save some." Wherever he traveled, he found ways to relate to the people around him. Paul didn't compromise his convictions or hide his faith in Jesus; instead, he sought to find points of connection—things they had in common. In Acts 17, when Paul spoke to a crowd of intellectual philosophers in Athens, Greece, he began by mentioning a statue he'd observed in the community, and he even quoted a Greek poet. Paul's familiarity with Athenian culture helped him make an initial connection that served as a springboard from which he preached a powerful message about Jesus.

Although your lifestyle won't fully mirror those of non-Christian teammates and friends, you can still find common ground. Just as Paul learned about Athenian culture, and Annabelle danced and sang along with her teammates' music, we can connect through books, music, movies, and social media, or through food, fashion, and hobbies.

God placed us in the world—his good world—to enjoy life with friends as we spread his light. We don't have to hold ourselves stiff and separate—we can laugh, dance, sing, and even eat our way to closer bonds and deeper friendships. You never know what surprising point of connection might give you a chance to share about God's love.

TAKE A KNEE

Lord, thank you for the privilege of sharing about you with friends. Please help me find ways to have fun and build friendships, and open my eyes to opportunities to share about you along the way. In Jesus's name, amen.

WEEKLY CHECK-IN

What went well this week? What was hard? Did I meet the goals I set for myself?

____

____

____

How is my body feeling? How is my heart feeling? How do I feel about my connection with God?

____

____

____

In what ways do I need support? How can I invite that support?

____

____

____

What do I want to pray about for next week? Who can I invite to pray with me and for me?

____

____

____

WEEK 8: COMPLICATIONS AND FRUSTRATIONS

Time-Out: My Hopes, Prayers, and Goals for This Week

"I think you have a stress fracture," said Dr. Jones.

Time stopped in the little room. The white walls pressed in, the fluorescent lights became too bright. Jaiya fought to find words. "What does that mean? I have to defend my title at nationals, I can't stop running now . . ."

"You'll have to stop or it won't heal. I'm sorry."

"For how long?" Jaiya asked, panic fluttering in her chest. "A few weeks? A month?"

"No running for at least three months," said Dr. Jones.

A buzzing filled Jaiya's ears. She hadn't taken three months off running in—well, ever. Running was her *life*.

"Can she bike?" Jaiya's dad asked. "She's got to do something to stay conditioned."

"Yes," said Dr. Jones. "I'll put you in touch with a physical therapist and . . ."

Their conversation faded into background noise as Jaiya tried to wrap her head around this setback. Three months off when she was supposed to be training for nationals? How could she possibly stay in running shape without *running*?

Two long months passed. Two months filled with biking and weight training, but no running. Every day, Jaiya met her training group at the gym. Warmed up with them, then wrestled an encouraging smile onto her face as her friends went outside to run together, and Jaiya rode a stationary bike indoors alone. Discouragement and jealousy knocked on the door of her heart, but she kept the door firmly shut. *God has a plan for them and a plan for you,* she reminded herself. *Just keep trusting and keep training.*

Several months after her stress fracture diagnosis, Jaiya's parents took her to a new doctor, a bone specialist. The doctor pointed at her X-rays. "I don't see a fracture," he said.

"What?" Jaiya and her parents exclaimed.

"No fracture," the doctor said with a smile.

Jaiya's thoughts started whirling. "So what does that mean?

Can I . . ." She hardly dared speak the words, afraid of being disappointed. "Can I start running again? Or do I still have to wait another month?"

"You can run," the doctor said.

Jaiya beamed as her parents gave little whoops of joy. But then fear fisted Jaiya's heart: *After two months off, can I get ready for nationals in time? I can't possibly come back as fast as I was last year . . . can I?*

Jaiya eased back into running, still being careful. Nationals were only weeks away . . . then days . . . then minutes.

Jaiya warmed up for her heat—this would be her first 400-meter race since her injury—and set up her blocks. A chorus of what-ifs ran through her head: *What if I'm not ready? What if I lose my title?*

She traded smiles with the other girls in her heat, who were stretching and jumping behind their blocks, staying loose. Jaiya took deep breaths, wishing she had a friend in this heat who could pray with her. Just then, a runner beside her spoke up: "Hey, girls, can we all pray together before we race?"

Jaiya's heart leapt. "I'd love to!"

All eight girls circled up, and as they prayed, Jaiya's thoughts cleared and her nerves calmed. She'd prayed with teammates many times, but never with a group of competitors like this: eight strangers from different teams, uniting in prayer to invite God into their race. In their unity, Jaiya felt God's presence and care.

The girls said amen just as the announcer called them to their blocks. As Jaiya set her feet, she thought about her favorite Scripture: "I can do all things through him who gives me strength." The God who had been with her throughout her recovery would be with her as she ran, no matter the outcome.

The starting gun fired, and Jaiya took off.

FINDING PATIENCE AND PERSPECTIVE DURING REHAB

The end of a matter is better than its beginning, and patience is better than pride.
Ecclesiastes 7:8

WARM-UP

Do you consider yourself a patient person? Why or why not?

Nobody wants to be injured. Nobody wants to stand on the sidelines watching everyone else work out while your muscles turn to mush. Nobody wants to be a spectator while the rest of the team competes.

This week we're going to study some verses that will help us handle the complications and frustrations we experience in sports—struggles like unfairness, pressure, conflict, overwhelm, and injury. If you relate to Jaiya's story and you're dealing with an injury, you don't need me to tell you the importance of taking time to rest and recover—your doctor and parents and coaches have probably already given the you-need-time-to-heal speech. But even when your head agrees, your heart can still feel frustrated.

Today's simple Scripture can help your perspective. Solomon begins by saying, "The end of a matter is better than its beginning." End goals matter, and endings are rewarding, right? The end goal of rest and rehab is healing so you can play again, but unfortunately, we first have to survive the rough beginning stages. At the start of your rehab, you may be wrestling with a lot of whys: *Why me? Why now? Why this?* You may want to rush the process, skip steps, or pretend your pain away. But you can't rush healing.

Solomon goes on to say, "Patience is better than pride." Let's be honest: Injury is rough on our pride. Injury can make us feel weak, overlooked, and unimportant. Injury forces us to accept advice we may not like. It forces us to trust physical therapists, doctors, and other specialists. Injury may reveal that our confidence and identity are too entangled in our sport, especially if we're feeling insecure and a bit lost: *If I'm not an athlete, who am I?*

If you're dealing with an injury, I pray you'll let today's Scripture guide your perspective and boost your patience. Focus on the end goal: complete recovery and a healthy body. The early stages of rest and rehab may be difficult—even miserable—but they'll pay off in the end. As Solomon said, the end will be better than the beginning. The end will be *worth* the beginning.

In Jaiya's first race after her injury, she crossed the finish line in first place, astounded. Her first thought was another prayer: *Thank you, Jesus, for being with me. Not just today, but during all the hard days leading up to this moment.*

As you work toward healing, ask God for patience. When pride tempts you to push for a hurry-up timeline, trust the experts who are guiding your recovery, and humbly embrace their advice. It'll be worth it in the end.

PRACTICE

Write down three benefits of taking time to rest after an injury.

1. ______________________________

____

2. ______________________________

____

3. ______________________________

____

THAT'S NOT FAIR

Be still in the presence of the LORD, and wait patiently for him to act. Don't worry about evil people who prosper or fret about their wicked schemes. Stop being angry! Turn from your rage! Do not lose your temper—it only leads to harm. For the wicked will be destroyed, but those who trust in the LORD will possess the land. . . . For the LORD loves justice, and he will never abandon the godly.
Psalm 37:7–9, 28 NLT

WARM-UP

What bothers you most about unfairness?

You probably figured out early on that sports aren't always fair. Unfairness can take many forms: injury, misfortune, mistreatment . . . and the list goes on. As a sophomore, Jaiya suffered an injury, and it felt unfair that she had to take time to recover while others continued training. As a freshman, I experienced a different kind of unfairness.

My JV basketball team wasn't just losing games; we were getting obliterated. Midway through the season, our coach started bringing in girls from the varsity volleyball team to play our games for us. They never came to our practices—they just showed up for competition, put on our uniforms, and played our games while we watched from the bench. The whole thing felt discouraging and unfair. Sure, the older volleyball players were great athletes who improved our record, but they also kept *us* from improving because we weren't getting game experience. The situation sent a strange message to me and my teammates: *It doesn't matter if you come to practice and work hard—I want to win, no matter what. Also, you stink.*

JV basketball was one of my first experiences with the profound unfairness we sometimes encounter in sports. When life is unfair and the wrong people get ahead, it can feel frustrating—even infuriating. Today, let's learn again from David, the giant-slaying shepherd who became Israel's king. He was no stranger to unfairness: Once the prophet Samuel anointed David, King Saul became jealous and wanted David dead. David spent years of his life hiding from Saul in the wilderness.

When David wrote Psalm 37, it seems he was wrestling with unfairness he saw in his own life and in the world: wicked people receiving praise and success while righteous people suffer; evil people prospering instead of being punished. His words remind us of a few key truths about life, God, and our attitudes:

- *The Lord loves justice.* Even if human authorities aren't paying attention or setting things right, God is watching. He loves justice and fairness, and he's working even when we can't see it.
- *Losing your temper only makes things worse.* Rage and resentment are a waste of energy. Not only do those emotions make us miserable, they may also lead us to say and do things we later regret.
- *Those who trust in the Lord will be blessed.* The wicked and unworthy won't prosper in the long run; God honors righteousness in the end.

If you're stuck in an unfair situation today, let David's words bring you comfort and hope. God is aware, he cares, and he is working.

PRACTICE

Write about an unfair situation you've experienced in the space below. Take it to God in prayer, asking him to set it right, if possible. Also ask him to give you a sense of peace if it remains unresolved.

____

____

____

UNDER PRESSURE

Saul son of Kish was chosen from among them. But when they looked for him, he had disappeared! So they asked the LORD, "Where is he?" And the LORD replied, "He is hiding among the baggage." So they found him and brought him out, and he stood head and shoulders above anyone else.
1 Samuel 10:21–23 NLT

WARM-UP

Do people's expectations motivate you or stress you out?

We've spent several devotions getting to know David, the man who became Israel's most beloved king. Let's back up a few years and meet the failed ruler David replaced: Israel's first king, Saul.

For many years, the nation of Israel had been begging God for a king, and God finally relented. God asked the prophet Samuel to appoint Saul, an impressive young man from the tribe of Benjamin. (Towering head and shoulders above everyone else, Saul would have made a great center on a basketball team.) Samuel called the people together to make the Big Announcement, and it went something like this:

Samuel cries out, "And the first king of Israel will be . . . Saul son of Kish!"

People cheer, confetti flies, but—Saul is a no-show.

Confetti flutters to the ground as confused silence falls over the crowd.

Samuel whispers to a nearby servant, "Quick, find Saul!"

After a lengthy search, a servant girl spots Saul's long legs peeking out from behind a pile of bags. Saul awkwardly un-pretzels himself and emerges from his hiding place with a sheepish grin.

This scene hints at the pressure Saul must have felt in being unexpectedly called to a new role. A public role where his every move would be on display for all to celebrate—or criticize. Maybe you know the feeling: All eyes on you, expectations sky-high, the weight of your world—your team, your school, your family—heavy on your shoulders. And not all pressure is external: When Jaiya returned to the track after her injury, she knew her supporters loved her no matter what, but as a driven athlete, she hoped to repeat her past success. Internal or external, the pressure to excel is enough to make anyone want to hide in the locker room.

Sadly, Saul crumbled under the pressures of kingship, and God took his throne away, giving it to David instead. Why did David succeed where Saul failed? Unlike Saul, David handled pressure and expectations by depending on God. In Psalm 27:1, David wrote, "The LORD is the stronghold of my life—of whom shall I be afraid?" The Lord was David's safe place, and David valued God's approval more than people's.

If you've ever felt overwhelmed by others' expectations or the pressure to succeed, and if you've ever been tempted to run away and hide like Saul did, take comfort from David's words: God is your safe place, and his love does not depend on your performance. You don't have to win a game or set a record to make God proud. He's already proud, and he loves you as you are.

TAKE A KNEE

Dear Lord, thank you for having great vision for my life but also for loving me just as I am today. It's reassuring to know that I don't have to earn your love or approval. Thank you for being my safe place. In Jesus's name, amen.

WHEN YOU SHOULDN'T LISTEN

Do not pay attention to every word people say, or you may hear your servant cursing you— for you know in your heart that many times you yourself have cursed others.
Ecclesiastes 7:21–22

WARM-UP

Do you consider yourself sensitive, or can you quickly shake off criticism?

After my daughter Cassidy's first four-year-old soccer game, she ran off the field, wide-eyed and confused: "Mommy, the game was fun, but why did the coach yell so much? Was he mad?" Laughing, I attempted to explain the concept of "sports yelling," and how *loud* isn't always the same thing as *mad*.

But what about times when sports yelling *is* angry yelling? Every athlete gets the occasional earful from coaches and teammates, and many of us have dished out some angry outbursts ourselves. Maybe we've mumbled something salty to a teammate under our breath like, "What a stupid move!" or we've lost it and shouted, "You always blow that play!" Once we calmed down, we probably felt like a jerk and wished we could take back our words. Those are the kind of scenarios today's Scripture is talking about.

At first glance, this passage is surprising. It's from the book of Ecclesiastes, which is traditionally credited to King Solomon. Solomon's book is unique because sometimes he writes ironically or from a worldly, cynical perspective. He tackles hard questions like, *Why is life unfair?, What really makes us happy?*, and *Why do bad things happen to good people?*

Solomon also offers a practical piece of advice to protect our relationships. He writes, "Do not pay attention to every word people say, or you may hear your servant cursing you—for you know in your heart that many times you yourself have cursed others." By *curse*, he isn't talking about four-letter words. He's talking about times when people "curse" each other by getting angry and speaking rashly. That's an experience we can all relate to: We've all hurt others with our words, and others have hurt us too.

Sports can get tense. Games become physical, coaches get heated, players grow feisty, parents lose their ever-loving minds. People say things they don't really mean and wouldn't normally say. In those moments, Solomon's wisdom can help us develop thicker skin, avoid hurt feelings and conflict, and move on quickly from tense moments.

So what's Solomon's advice? In modern terms, he might say, "Let's be honest: We all have moments when we say things we shouldn't say. So let some salty comments slide. Don't take every insult personally."

Passionate competitors sometimes become too passionate. In the heat of the moment, people say dumb things that are out of character. Resilient athletes know when to listen . . . and when to let things go.

PRACTICE

On a separate piece of paper, write down a situation you need to forget about. Pray about letting it go, then crumple up the paper and throw it away.

ASK A BETTER QUESTION

Do not say, "Why were the old days better than these?" For it is not wise to ask such questions.
Ecclesiastes 7:10

WARM-UP

If you could relive one sports season without changing anything, which season would you want to experience all over again?

Sometimes we torment ourselves with unanswerable questions. These questions don't lead to resolutions—only to anxiety and fear. They often begin with the words *why* and *what if*. For example, when Jaiya was injured, she had to resist the temptation to dwell on questions like, "Why is this happening to me?" and "What if I don't fully recover?" In Ecclesiastes, Solomon brings up another unanswerable question: "Why were the old days better than these?"

How tempting it is to look back on happier, easier times, longing to go back. As an athlete, you might ask yourself questions like, *Why can't I go back to last season when we had such a strong team? Why can't the coach I loved still be here? Why can't I be healthy like I was last year?* If you're dealing with a change, an injury, or a setback, you probably have a lot of *why* questions, questions without satisfying answers. The queen of all such questions is, *Why me?*

Unfortunately, no one can answer that question. We can ask God *why* all day long—and he's certainly willing to listen and wrap his arms around us, shouldering our grief and pain—but it's unlikely we're going to hear a voice from heaven offering the explanation we crave. Sadly, the setback happened. Asking why doesn't change the facts. Solomon's practical advice in Ecclesiastes is essentially this: *Don't waste energy dwelling on frustrating questions that only make you more miserable.*

But it's not enough to simply avoid negative thoughts and questions. In Romans 12:21, Paul counseled, "Overcome evil with good." We can overcome the "evil" of discouragement and frustration by replacing negative thoughts with good thoughts. Positive thoughts. Productive thoughts. For example, we can turn *Why me?* into *What next?*

What next? is a productive question because it helps us focus on our next action step. It reminds us that we're not helpless. We can move forward. We can't control what happened *to* us in the past, but we can control what happens *in* us—what we do in this moment.

The next time you're tempted to dwell on setbacks, obsessing over frustrating, unanswerable questions, try taking Solomon's advice. Take charge of your thoughts. Focus on what you *can* do. Ask yourself, *What's next?*

DRILL

What's the next thing you need to do to grow as an athlete?

WHEN SPORTS KEEP YOU AWAY FROM CHURCH

And let us be concerned about one another in order to promote love and good works, not staying away from our worship meetings, as some habitually do, but encouraging each other, and all the more as you see the day drawing near.
Hebrews 10:24–25 HCSB

WARM-UP

What's your favorite part of church service?

My girl Avery looked up at me, teary-eyed. "Mom, our game got moved to Wednesday. I'll miss youth group again." She tipped her head back, as if trying to make the tears drain back into her eyes. "I just—I really need to hear a Bible lesson. And I miss my friends."

"Could you make it to youth group for the last fifteen minutes?" I asked.

"That could work," Avery said, perking up—then wrinkling her nose. "I'll be gross and sweaty though."

I grinned. "Your friends are used to that by now."

Avery socked me in the shoulder.

Does this scenario sound familiar? The pressures of your season probably have you feeling stretched and stressed, longing for encouragement. At a time when you need Christian friendship and fellowship the most, you have the least amount of time for them.

In today's passage, the writer of Hebrews reminds us to encourage one another in our Christian walk. He urges us not to habitually miss worship meetings, as they provide opportunities for growth and relationship. In theory, we all amen that passage, right? *Yes, I need Christian community! Godly friends keep me inspired!* But sometimes the in-season schedule gets so complex that it's tempting to throw in the towel on youth group and church.

But what if there's another option? A creative solution that fulfills your obligations to your team while also fulfilling your own needs for spiritual friendship and nourishment? No solution will be perfect, but a little fellowship is better than none. Like Avery, you might have to get creative, making the most of brief windows of time. Here are a few strategies that may help:

- Be open with your youth pastor or spiritual mentor about your schedule and needs. Share your desire to stay connected even when your attendance is less consistent.
- Invite your youth group or godly friends to your meets and games.
- Ask for prayer support for especially busy weeks or big competitions.
- Start a text thread with Christian friends where you share Scriptures, prayers, and encouragement.
- Ask a godly teammate to be a prayer partner during the season.

While you're in season you'll probably have to miss some worship services and fellowship times, but there's no need to stress or feel guilty. God is with you and for you, wherever you are. He's not up in heaven keeping track of church attendance on a big chart. Just make sure that missing church connections doesn't become a *habit*, a new lifestyle that persists even after the season ends.

Let's remember, we don't go to church solely for our own benefit. Your godly friends need you as much as you need them. They'll welcome you to church with enthusiastic hugs even if you show up late, still damp and glistening from an after-practice shower. They'll even welcome you if you show up all sweaty and gross—they just might skip the hugs.

DRILL

Choose one of the strategies above and put it into practice this week.

WHEN YOUR FUTURE IS UNCERTAIN

I will lead the blind by ways they have not known, along unfamiliar paths I will guide them; I will turn the darkness into light before them and make the rough places smooth. These are the things I will do; I will not forsake them.
Isaiah 42:16

WARM-UP

How do you handle uncertainty?

Michelle rushed toward the pool, late for her heat. Coach jogged beside her, spouting last-minute reminders. Nodding, Michelle reached for her goggles, which were dangling from Coach's fingers. But he flicked the goggles away, off into the bleachers.

"Oops!" Coach flashed a teasing grin that clearly said, *Not oops. I did that on purpose.*

Michelle's jaw dropped.

"Why'd you do that? I'll be blind in the water!"

Coach was already walking away. "I want you to learn to count your strokes. To trust your training even when you can't see."

Michelle stepped onto her starting block. The gun went off, and she dove in.

Sometimes coaches do things that don't make sense. They put us in uncomfortable situations that test our trust in our training—and in them. That day, Michelle's coach taught her an unconventional lesson: Sometimes you have to race blind. You need to swim on faith that your training will see you through, even with limited vision.

In a similar way, God sometimes "coaches" us through life by allowing us to face confusing, uncertain, or uncomfortable situations. And in life, we always swim into the future with limited vision. Our future always has question marks:

How will this season go?
Will I recover from this injury?
Will a college coach make me an offer?

Many centuries ago, God spoke through the prophet Isaiah to comfort his people during uncertain times. He said, "I will lead the blind by ways they have not known, along unfamiliar paths I will guide them." Even when we are blind, God can see. We may be unfamiliar with our path, unable to discern what lies over the next hill, but God sees. God knows. And he is guiding us.

His promise gets even better: "I will turn the darkness into light before them and make the rough places smooth . . . I will not forsake them." God shines a light when our path feels dark, he eases our journey when it grows rocky, and he never leaves us alone.

If you've been stressing about your season or your future, take your worries to God. Even though you can't see what lies ahead, he can. Like a good coach, God knows what he's doing, where he's leading you, and how to prepare you for the challenges to come.

Michelle's unusual training moment with her coach came into play years later when she was competing in one of the most important races of her life. When she dove in, her goggles filled with water, completely blinding her. She flashed back to that day when Coach threw away her goggles, and she knew what to do: *Count your strokes. Trust your training.*

She won the race.

TAKE A KNEE

Father, thank you that you can see around every blind turn, and you are never surprised. Thank you for guiding me through uncertainties. I ask for wisdom in making decisions and a sense of peace as I wait for you to reveal what's next. I trust you and I love you. In Jesus's name, amen.

WEEKLY CHECK-IN

What went well this week? What was hard? Did I meet the goals I set for myself?

____

____

____

How is my body feeling? How is my heart feeling? How do I feel about my connection with God?

____

____

____

In what ways do I need support? How can I invite that support?

____

____

____

What do I want to pray about for next week? Who can I invite to pray with me and for me?

____

____

____

WEEK 9: CHRISTLIKE COMPETITORS

Time-Out: My Hopes, Prayers, and Goals for This Week

"I want to graduate early," Emily said, not quite looking the dean in the eye across his ginormous desk.

He leaned back, studying her; his chair squeaked as if to protest Emily's decision. "But what about your senior year on the field hockey team?"

There it was—the question Emily had been afraid he would ask. She took a deep breath, and out poured the truth: "I'm not going to play—I'll just be standing on the sidelines all year." She didn't explain all the other reasons:

Because anxiety got the better of me last year, and I didn't play my best.

Because standing on the sidelines as a senior is embarrassing.

Because this isn't what my last season was supposed to look like.

Because I'm tired of fighting.

The dean placed his elbows on the desk, steepling his fingers together against his lips. When he didn't speak, Emily filled the empty space with nervous words. "Besides, I'm going to medical school, so . . . I might as well get my life going." She heard the defensiveness in her own voice, the please-don't-ask-anymore-questions tone.

"Emily, are you a Christian?"

Emily's mouth fell open in surprise. This was Boston, not the religious South she'd grown up in. Around here, faith felt like a don't-ask-don't-tell kind of topic. It had certainly never come up with a professor before.

Emily looked the dean in the eye. "Yes. Yes, I am."

"I thought so." He leaned forward. "Emily, what if God wants you to stay here?"

"W-what?" Emily couldn't have been more surprised if the dean had asked her to play field hockey on top of his desk.

"What if God has plans for your senior year that you can't even imagine? Plans that have nothing to do with whether you play a single game or stop a single goal? You and I both know there aren't many Christians on your team, so surely God has you here for a reason."

"But—but it's going to be a miserable year," Emily said. "I might not play at all."

The dean tapped a finger on his desk, speaking passionately. "Think about Jesus carrying his cross up to Calvary, on his way to be crucified. There was nothing in it for Jesus—nothing good. It was all suffering and shame. But if he hadn't made that sacrifice . . ."

"We didn't have a chance," Emily whispered, feeling tears prickle behind her eyes.

"Exactly. Jesus didn't go to the cross for himself—he did it for us. And I think God wants you to stay to shine a light for your team. You have teammates who may never hear about Jesus during college if not from you. And just imagine the example you can set for them, showing what humility, courage, and resilience look like, even if it's on the sidelines. You can model a Christlike spirit for girls who haven't seen it before. And who knows? Maybe that's why God brought you here—not for field hockey, but for the example you could set even through your heartache. For the girls you could reach for him."

Tears were streaming down Emily's face now. Every word the dean spoke was a knock on the door of her heart, and now the door stood wide open, ready to let faith inside. A godly perspective. A new attitude.

As Emily left the dean's office, she called her mom, hands shaking.

"How'd it go?" Mom asked. "Did you get your early graduation all figured out?

"I'm not graduating early," Emily said, hardly believing the words coming out of her mouth. "I've realized God's not done with me on this team. He has more for me to do."

Her mom spoke after a long silence. "But you're going to stand on the sidelines all season. Has something changed?"

"Well, nothing has changed with field hockey," Emily said. "I'm still not going to play. But something *has* changed—and that something is me."

BE AN INITIATOR

Jesus answered her, "If you knew the gift of God and who it is that asks you for a drink, you would have asked him and he would have given you living water."
John 4:10

WARM-UP

What's your go-to icebreaker question?

Emily wanted to help her teammates come to know Christ, and as her faith and confidence grew, so did her influence for the Lord. It's not always easy to have a Christlike influence—like Emily, we tend to grow into it over time. This week as we read about Jesus's life, relationships, and ministry, we'll identify some ways we can imitate him and shine a brighter light as we grow.

Jesus was an expert conversationalist. He had a way of taking quick encounters and making them powerful and memorable. He could turn a first-time interaction into a life-changing connection. In John 4, we read about a deep conversation Jesus had with a woman at a well. This conversation never should have happened, for several reasons. First, men and women from Jesus's culture didn't usually speak to each other in public unless they were family members. But Jesus respected and valued women and welcomed them into his ministry. Second, this woman was a Samaritan, and most Jews despised Samaritans and refused to associate with them. Third, this woman had a difficult past, and most devout Jews would have run the other way from a sinful soul like her.

Not Jesus. Not only did Jesus initiate a conversation with this woman; he quickly moved past the shallow small talk to reach her heart.

If you're looking to have a Christlike influence on your team, Jesus's example offers a few insights. In verse ten, Jesus threw out a surprising statement that got the woman intrigued: "If you knew the gift of God and who it is that asks you for a drink, you would have asked him and he would have given you living water."

Perhaps we can follow Jesus's example by mentioning our faith in the middle of everyday conversations. During her last year on the field hockey team, Emily sprinkled little comments about the Lord into her conversations, hoping to spark her teammates' curiosity. Sometimes those comments opened up an opportunity to share about God.

After Jesus's conversation with the Samaritan woman, she came to believe he was the Messiah, the Savior. She sprinted back to town and invited everyone to come meet him. Many Samaritans came to faith because of her testimony—and Jesus's courage in initiating their conversation.

A single moment can make a world of difference. Sometimes God takes one baby-brave step on our part—a deeper question, an honest answer, a mention of prayer—and uses it to change a life.

DRILL

Write down three questions you could ask that might take a conversation deeper with a teammate or friend.

1. ______________________________

____

____

2. ______________________________

____

____

3. ______________________________

____

____

BE A VISIONARY

The first thing Andrew did was to find his brother Simon and tell him, "We have found the Messiah" (that is, the Christ). And he brought him to Jesus. Jesus looked at him and said, "You are Simon son of John. You will be called Cephas" (which, when translated, is Peter).
John 1:41–42

WARM-UP

What's the weirdest nickname you've ever heard (or had)?

If the conversation depicted in today's verse had happened in a modern setting, I picture it playing out something like this:

Andrew is bouncing on the balls of his feet, excitement pouring off him in almost visible waves. "Simon, this is the preacher I told you about. Jesus, this is my brother Simon."

Jesus tips his head to one side, his dark eyes crinkled in amusement. "Right now, you call yourself Simon, the son of John. But that name isn't right. Too boring. I'm going to call you Peter."

"Huh?" Simon asks, utterly confused.

Jesus nods. "In Greek, Peter means *rock*. So . . . your new name is Rock Johnson. It's perfect." Jesus gives a satisfied grin, then smacks Peter on the shoulder. "Let's get to work—time to grow into that name."

I wonder how Simon Peter felt in this moment. Probably a bit confused—but also inspired. The moment they met, Jesus offered Peter a new vision for his life. He looked straight into Peter's soul and saw past the emotional, all-over-the-place fisherman he was that day to the bold, dependable leader he could become. All Simon needed was to spend time with Jesus.

(Also, can we pause to acknowledge that the apostle Peter was the *original* Rock Johnson?)

Jesus is a visionary. He sees the people we are today, weaknesses and all, and he envisions the people we can become. He sees *all* our potential. And the more time we spend with him, the more we grow into that potential.

That means whatever weaknesses we have today can transform under Jesus's influence. They might even become our strengths.

The tricky emotions we struggle to master today don't have to stay problematic forever—Jesus can help us gain emotional strength and health.

Perhaps best of all, we can be a visionary for others. We can do for friends and teammates what Jesus has done for us. That's what Emily's dean did for her when he helped her figure out the role she could fill her senior season, and then what Emily herself learned to do that year: She supported her teammates from the sidelines and pointed them toward the Lord.

Just imagine what Jesus could do with the talents and passions of the girls on your team. Even if they aren't yet interested in giving their hearts to Jesus, he knows who they could become. Jesus's faith in Peter changed his character and his destiny, and Jesus's faith in us is just as powerful. As we spend time with the Lord, he'll help us grow into his vision for us. A vision that's more than just game-changing—it's life-changing.

PRACTICE

Choose a girl on your team whose strengths you admire, and encourage her today.

BE AN INFLUENCER

Now while he was in Jerusalem at the Passover Festival, many people saw the signs he was performing and believed in his name. But Jesus would not entrust himself to them, for he knew all people. He did not need any testimony about mankind, for he knew what was in each person.
John 2:23–25

WARM-UP

How would you describe your team's vibe?

Week three, junior year cross-country season. I was still new to the team and to running, but after a few weeks I'd learned the names and moved past the agonizing, can-barely-walk level of soreness. I'd also learned that the faster you ran, the cooler you were.

"Okay, ladies, today we're running the four-mile loop," Coach said. "Get going!"

The team quickly self-sorted into groups. I joined a group I hoped wasn't too fast and watched with a twinge of envy as the cool girls sped ahead, laughing and looking like the fastest of runners *and* the best of friends. As my group jogged onto the trail, I admitted something to myself: *I really want the cool girls to like me.*

We all want to feel welcomed and needed on our teams, like we have a part to play. Emily and I both longed to feel valuable, and we struggled to find our place when we weren't having the success we wanted. Feeling valuable and accepted isn't just about making athletic contributions; every team has a distinct vibe, a group personality. Each team determines what belonging and "coolness" are, based on different values. Some teams value humor and extroversion, so the funniest, loudest girls are the center of the in-crowd. Some teams prize intensity, drive, and achievement, so the most successful athletes are the most popular. Other teams are the opposite: Their laid-back vibe means the chill, too-cool-to-care girls are the cool ones. (Ironic, right?) If someone works too hard (and makes everyone else look bad), other girls roll their eyes and call her a try-hard. Navigating these dynamics can be confusing. In our eagerness to find friends, it can be tempting to change ourselves to fit the team vibe.

Jesus's example can guide us as we negotiate team dynamics and seek to make friends. Early in his ministry, Jesus was gaining both followers and attention. At first, much of that attention was positive. People were amazed by his teachings and miracles, and many put their faith in him. But being temporarily popular didn't turn Jesus's head. John writes, "Jesus would not entrust himself to them, for he knew all people."

Jesus didn't draw his confidence or self-esteem from people's opinions—he drew them from God. Why did he take this view? Because "he knew what was in each person." Jesus loved people, but he knew they could be unpredictable, unreliable. So he entrusted himself to God alone. He didn't need people to like him or approve of him. God liked him and approved of him, and that was enough. Jesus didn't let the world influence him—he chose to be an influencer who showed others the way.

People aren't always a safe place for our self-esteem, but God always is. People aren't always loving, but God always is. Let's seek his approval and ask him who he wants us to influence today.

PRACTICE

In what ways do you already have influence on your team? How would you like to influence others moving forward? Journal some thoughts in the space below.

____

____

____

BE INCLUSIVE

When Jesus reached the spot, he looked up and said to him, "Zacchaeus, come down immediately. I must stay at your house today." So he came down at once and welcomed him gladly. All the people saw this and began to mutter, "He has gone to be the guest of a sinner."
Luke 19:5–7

WARM-UP

What makes you feel included?

In Jesus's day, tax collectors often did not have great reputations. Other Jews tended to view them as traitors who had betrayed their own people by going to work for the Roman government, aka the enemy. Tax collectors were notorious for being dishonest cheats who charged taxpayers money in addition to the Roman taxes they were hired to collect; basically, they got rich by scamming their neighbors. Many pious Jews would have nothing to do with tax collectors—they wouldn't set foot in their houses or even eat with them.

In Luke 19, we read about a tax collector named Zacchaeus who was eager to hear Jesus's preaching. Because Zacchaeus was a short man (no basketball career for this guy), he had to climb a tree in order to see over the crowd. Jesus, sensing an open heart, stopped underneath the tree and singled Zacchaeus out—in fact, Jesus invited himself to eat dinner at the tax collector's house.

Others who saw this invitation grumbled and criticized. How dare Jesus reach out to someone so unrighteous, so untouchable? Jesus must not be very righteous himself if he was willing to associate with someone like Zacchaeus.

But Zacchaeus was so moved that he repented on the spot, giving half his possessions to the poor and offering to pay back anyone he'd cheated.

Jesus was delighted. He said, "Today salvation has come to this house, because this man, too, is a son of Abraham" (v. 9).

Jesus's inclusiveness brought salvation to a man everyone else had written off. Zacchaeus was uncool, unrighteous, and uninvited everywhere—except with Jesus. But Jesus knew that Zacchaeus's history of bad decisions didn't have to define his future. Zacchaeus just needed a chance. An invitation. And so Jesus gave him one.

Most of Emily's teammates hadn't grown up going to church, so she prayed that God would use her life to make other girls curious about faith. She offered simple invitations to girls who seemed open to the Lord: Sometimes she shared a Scripture; other times she invited them to a Bible study. Even if they never showed interest in God, she tried to make everyone feel loved just as Jesus had done for Zacchaeus.

Zacchaeus wasn't the only outsider Jesus befriended. Jesus broke every imaginable barrier, reaching out to the sinful, the sick, and the second-class. He reached out to women, children, foreigners, the elderly, and the unpopular.

As we strive to imitate Christ, let's open our eyes to notice the outsiders at school and on our teams. Let's open our mouths to say, "Want to sit with me? Warm up with me? Train with me?" Let's open our friend groups—and our hearts—to include everyone we can.

PRACTICE

How can you imitate Jesus's heart of inclusivity on your team? Who can you help pull into the group?

____

____

____

____

____

____

BE MERCIFUL

When Jesus landed and saw a large crowd, he had compassion on them, because they were like sheep without a shepherd. So he began teaching them many things.
Mark 6:34

WARM-UP

When has a friend shown you compassion or forgiveness?

Toya laced up her cleats, wishing she had headphones to drown out the locker room conversations around her. In one corner, someone was blasting music with an awesome bass beat but violent lyrics. In another corner, a group of her teammates was laughing at a video of some poor freshman tripping in the hallway. Toya felt anger bubbling up, but she reminded herself: *Without Jesus, I'd be doing all the same things.* I have *done all the same things. I just need to model a different way. Jesus's way.* The thought helped, softening her irritation and sparking her compassion.

The world's standards of right and wrong are often different than Jesus's standards—sometimes dramatically so. The world has different definitions of gossip, friendship, kindness, and even basic manners. When we encounter those differences, we may be tempted to feel frustrated or even judgmental. One reason Jesus came to earth was to show us how to live in a lost and broken world. How to love when it's hard. How to show mercy when it hurts.

In Mark 6, Jesus has just heard the devastating news that his relative John the Baptist has been beheaded. Needing time to grieve in private, Jesus left town and crossed the Sea of Galilee with his disciples, but when they landed, a crowd was already waiting for them. How did Jesus respond? With mercy and generosity. He saw the people not as needy and demanding, but as they really were: harassed and helpless. They were lost sheep desperate for a loving shepherd to lead them. And so Jesus did exactly that. He put his needs on hold so he could meet theirs. (And *this*—this staggering selflessness—is why we worship Jesus!)

We catch another glimpse of Jesus's merciful compassion in Matthew 11:28–29, when he said, "Come to me all you who are weary and burdened, and I will give you rest. Take my yoke upon you and learn from me, for I am gentle and humble in heart, and you will find rest for your souls." Jesus saw all the heartache people carried, and *he* ached to draw people close.

If you sometimes feel upset by the brokenness around you, ask God to help you see the world with Jesus's eyes. Jesus didn't only see people's sin; he also saw the pain that produced the sin—he viewed the world with conviction *and* compassion. Yes, people are lost, confused, and sometimes unkind. *This is why they need Jesus*—and why Jesus needs us, his followers. Now that he's gone, we are his compassionate eyes, his loving arms.

How can you show mercy today?

EXTRA REP

"But God had mercy on me so that Christ Jesus could use me as a prime example of his great patience with even the worst sinners. Then others will realize that they, too, can believe in him and receive eternal life" (1 Timothy 1:16 NLT).

BE A SERVANT

"Do you understand what I have done for you?" [Jesus] asked them. "You call me 'Teacher' and 'Lord,' and rightly so, for that is what I am. Now that I, your Lord and Teacher, have washed your feet, you also should wash one another's feet."
John 13:12–14

WARM-UP

What is your team's least favorite chore?

Jesus lived in the pre-Nike days. With the Cool Sneaker Trend still two millennia away, most people wore leather sandals to protect their feet from the dusty desert roads. As you might imagine, in Jesus's culture, foot aroma was an issue. Foot hygiene was a thing. When you entered someone's home, they would welcome you by having their servants wash your feet. This was considered an essential act of hospitality.

Here in John 13, several hours before Jesus was arrested, he performed a memorable act of service for his disciples. After dinner, he wrapped a towel around his waist, just like a servant would, and he washed his disciples' feet. He intentionally made himself the least important person in the room, performing a menial task far beneath his station.

Most of his disciples sat in stunned silence, accepting this strange gift—except Peter. Peter couldn't help but object, and Jesus had to explain his purpose. Jesus concluded the lesson by encouraging his disciples to imitate his heart of service. If Jesus—God in the flesh, the greatest of all—was not too great to serve, then who are we to avoid humble service? Like Jesus, we are called to put others first, to humble ourselves, and to serve generously without complaining.

We are called to serve everyone we love in this way: family, friends, neighbors, teammates.

What would it look like for you to serve your team? Every team has menial tasks no one wants to do: Arriving early to set up equipment. Staying late to break down and clean up. Sweeping the locker room. Cleaning equipment. Carrying bags.

The world's wisdom says, "Those tasks are for the worst players, the girls who haven't earned their starting position yet. Once you've established yourself as a valuable player or leader, you don't have to do the grunt work anymore. And if you're a senior, forget about helping—now it's your turn to sit back and let the freshmen do the hard stuff."

That may be the way the world works, but it's not the attitude Jesus modeled and taught. Jesus's wisdom says, "The greater you are, the more you serve." His example calls us to continue serving no matter what year we are or what role we play. In Emily's case, inspired by the Lord's humility, she embraced a supporting role during her senior season, offering her enthusiasm and encouragement even though she wasn't competing on the field as often.

Our humble acts of service are acts of devotion we offer to Jesus. Even if no one else sees us serving, Jesus sees. And if no one thanks us, that's okay—we're not serving because we want to be thanked. We're serving as an expression of love for the Lord, and love for the ones we are serving. That knowledge is thanks enough.

PRACTICE

Remember that chore you listed in the warm-up? Consider volunteering to do it this week.

BE BACKWARD

The Pharisees, who dearly loved their money, heard all this and scoffed at him. Then he said to them, "You like to appear righteous in public, but God knows your hearts. What this world honors is detestable in the sight of God."
Luke 16:14–15 NLT

WARM-UP

When do you feel most out of place or uncomfortable?

Lana tossed her bag into the trunk, then slumped into the passenger seat beside her mom.

Mom's eyebrows climbed her forehead. "Bad practice?"

"Not exactly, I just . . . I feel weird. Everyone kept going off about how bad the refs were last night. I mean, they're not wrong, the refs were biased, but today it felt like everyone was having a competition to see who could cuss them out with the most—uh, *creative* language."

"Oh boy."

"Yeah. And it was like, the more colorful it got, the more everyone laughed and cheered. It just . . . it felt backward."

Sometimes the world celebrates the wrong things: Unkindness. Anger. Resentment. Sensuality. Rough language. This is not a new problem. The world has been getting things backward since the beginning. Jesus once confronted some religious people who claimed to love God but had their priorities wrong: They valued money more than generosity. Jesus tried to correct their thinking by telling them, "What this world honors is detestable in the sight of God."

Psalm 12 talks about this conundrum when it says, "Therefore, LORD, we know you will protect the oppressed, preserving them forever from this lying generation, even though the wicked strut about, and evil is praised throughout the land" (vv. 7–8 NLT). The world praises people God would not. And the world celebrates sinful things, calling them cool, innovative, bold, and good. Every day, we have to choose whose perspective to believe: the world's or God's.

If you sometimes feel out of place in worldly situations, there's nothing wrong with you. In fact, feeling out of place is a good sign that you're living God's way. Why? Because God's way is countercultural.

Living God's way might mean you have to release the idea of being cool. My parents used to tell me, "You will probably have to choose between being popular and being respected. It's tough for Christians to be both."

Friends may not understand why you are different. Why you step out of cruel conversations. Why you don't jam to explicit songs on the team playlist. Why, like Lana, you keep your mouth shut instead of mouthing off, even when you have a right to be mad. Or why, like Emily, you choose a positive attitude even when you're disappointed about your role. Friends may not understand you, and they might not crown you the Coolest Girl on the Team, but chances are, they will respect you. They'll know you are different—and that you are different because you love God.

Just remember: The world has its priorities turned around. But as a Christlike competitor, it's okay to get things backward.

EXTRA REP

"All these people died still believing what God had promised them. . . . They agreed that they were foreigners and nomads here on earth. Obviously people who say such things are looking forward to a country they can call their own. If they had longed for the country they came from, they could have gone back. But they were looking for a better place, a heavenly homeland. That is why God is not ashamed to be called their God, for he has prepared a city for them" (Hebrews 11:13–16 NLT).

WEEKLY CHECK-IN

What went well this week? What was hard? Did I meet the goals I set for myself?

How is my body feeling? How is my heart feeling? How do I feel about my connection with God?

In what ways do I need support? How can I invite that support?

What do I want to pray about for next week? Who can I invite to pray with me and for me?

WEEK 10: HANDLING SPORTY FEELINGS

Time-Out: My Hopes, Prayers, and Goals for This Week

All the Feels: Alexis's Story

Alexis lay in bed blinking at the ceiling. Her brain was draped in half dreams, the room shrouded in early-morning gray. *What do I have today? Today is . . . Oh no. Today is Thursday. Tumbling day.*

Suddenly wide awake, her mind flashed back to last week's tumbling session. She'd been working on her back handspring. (Was she ever *not* working on her back handspring?) She'd twisted sideways and nearly landed on her face. Her shoulder pulsed with remembered pain. *C'mon, Alexis, toughen up. Tumbling is hard, but you love everything else about cheer. Get up and get going.* She lurched out of bed to get ready for class.

At school, Alexis did her best to be friendly to people around her—even when she wasn't cheering, she tried to be outgoing and caring—but the upcoming tumbling session hovered like a dark shadow, haunting her day.

She muscled through the afternoon, then dressed for tumbling. Looking in the mirror, Alexis sighed in frustration. Her hair was coiling up, rebelling against her efforts to straighten it into the kind of ponytail everyone on the team always wore. Uniformity mattered in cheer, but with her curvy hips, brown skin, and textured ponytail, Alexis wasn't . . . uniform. Insecurity climbed into her heart, elbowing anxiety aside to make room.

Alexis squared her shoulders and offered her reflection a you've-got-this smile, then grabbed her keys and headed out. At the gym, most of the team had gathered in the main area to work on advanced stunts. Alexis trailed behind a group of five girls who, like her, were still working on handsprings.

At least we train behind a wall of mats, so when I break my nose, only a few people will see, she thought with a wry grin. An internal voice piped up: "Alexis, you're being negative. Too worried about what everyone thinks. Besides, this team is supportive—everyone wants you to succeed."

I know, she argued with the voice. *But my brain and my emotions are not in sync today.*

Okay, time-out. If she was arguing with an inner voice, it was time to seek intervention. She searched the gym, found the friend she was looking for, and pulled her aside.

"Hey, Ellie, you know tumbling is my *favorite*," Alexis began, inserting heavy irony into the word as Ellie gave a knowing laugh, "and I'm kinda spiraling. Will you pray with me?"

Ellie darted in to give Alexis a quick hug. "Of course."

As they prayed, Alexis's heart made space for more feelings: gratitude and affection. Who knew one heart could cram so much inside?

The prayer had taken the teeth out of her fear, but it wasn't gone. As Alexis waited her turn, she obliterated the side of her thumb with nervous nibbling.

Her turn at last. She stepped up to the mat.

The group offered encouragement: "You've got this!" "Let's go!"

Alexis felt a surge of confidence. Her teammates were true cheerleaders, genuinely cheering each other on. What a gift. Breathing a quick prayer for safety, focusing on gratitude instead of fear, Alexis bent her knees and sprang.

AN ANTIDOTE FOR ANXIETY

Don't worry about anything; instead, pray about everything. Tell God what you need, and thank him for all he has done. Then you will experience God's peace, which exceeds anything we can understand. His peace will guard your hearts and minds as you live in Christ Jesus.
Philippians 4:6–7 NLT

WARM-UP

What are you worried about today?
What are you thankful for?

Sports can strap us into an emotional roller coaster ride: exhilarating highs, how-can-I-possibly-survive-this lows, and shocking twists that nearly give us whiplash. Like Alexis, we sometimes cycle through a huge range of feelings in a single day. This week we'll address some of the difficult emotions that can accompany sports, such as anger, fear, envy, and anxiety.

Sports can produce a lot of anxiety. By "a lot," I mean the can't-eat-can't-sleep-for-days-before-the-big-game kind of anxiety. And it's not just competitions that cause stress. Every time Alexis had tumbling practice, a knot of nerves tried to strangle her peace all day long. Some measure of anxiety is normal—it's how our minds and bodies get amped up to perform. A moderate dose of nerves produces adrenaline, which helps us focus and compete. But too much anxiety becomes all-consuming and may hurt our performance.

How do you feel when you read Paul's words in today's verse, "Don't worry about anything"? Honestly, my first thought is, *That's not realistic. I can't just push an off button in my brain. I've tried praying about my worries, but when I say amen, they're still there.*

But let's give Paul's advice a closer look. First, he tells us to pray *instead of* worrying. Every time anxiety hits, we're invited to redirect fear into prayer. It's doubly comforting to invite a friend to pray with us like Alexis did. Our prayer might sound like this: "Lord, I'm anxious about my upcoming event. Please be with me, easing my fears and helping me to perform my best with no regrets."

But wait—there's something missing from that prayer. Paul says, "Tell God what you need, *and thank him for all he has done*." When I'm stressed, gratitude isn't usually at the top of my prayer list. I'm so worry-focused that I don't remember to thank God.

What if we followed Paul's advice and added gratitude to our stressed-out prayer? The new version might sound like this: "Father, thank you for caring about this situation and knowing what is best for me. I'm grateful that you are working and that you are with me."

Praying with gratitude does something different inside us. Our anxiety may not disappear, but it does dial down a notch. Our hearts settle, remembering that God cares and he's with us. That knowledge brings a measure of peace, just like Paul promises: "You will experience God's peace . . . [which will] guard your hearts and minds" (v. 7).

PRACTICE

Spend a few minutes praying, challenging yourself to devote the first half of your prayer to thanksgiving.

WATCH YOUR TEMPER, WATCH YOUR WORDS

A gentle answer turns away anger, but a harsh word stirs up wrath. The tongue of the wise makes knowledge attractive, but the mouth of fools blurts out foolishness.
Proverbs 15:1–2 CSB

WARM-UP

How do you express anger?

"Foul! Number twenty-three!"

A crowd of parents roared disagreement from the stands.

Tosha gaped at the ref, furious. Words clawed their way up her throat—*Are you blind? That was a charge!*—and she opened her mouth to start yelling.

But then she spotted Coach, shaking her head and pressing her palms toward the ground, like, *Keep a lid on it*. "Stay cool, Tosha!" Coach called.

Tosha swallowed her words, but her blood still boiled.

Passionate players play passionately. You pour your heart into your sport, leaving it all on the court, the field, the mat. Like Alexis, you give your best not only because you care about excellence, but because you care about your team—your friends. At big competitions, emotions run high. Coaches get feisty. Players get spicy. Parents lose it completely.

Ever blurted out your anger at a referee, a player, or (gulp) your own coach—then immediately regretted it? Today's verse says, "A gentle answer turns away anger, but a harsh word stirs up wrath. The tongue of the wise makes knowledge attractive, but the mouth of fools blurts out foolishness." When we give anger its way, we say things we wouldn't normally say. And when we add harsh words to an already heated situation, it's like pouring gasoline onto a bonfire. The whole situation burns dangerously hot. And speaking of fires, think about this: When a player or coach yells at an official, it always backfires. Have you ever seen a yelled-at ref pause the game and say, "Oh wow, you're right! Thank you for pointing out my error!" Not only does the ref *not* change the call—they might kick the shouter out of the game.

Gentleness is the fire extinguisher that cools down heated situations. All it takes is one player saying, "My bad, sorry," or one coach calling, "Let's move on," and tension drains from the air. With nothing to feed on, the fire fizzles out.

The next time emotions start sparking, remember the Bible's wisdom: Watch your temper, watch your words . . . and watch things go better in the end.

EXTRA REP

Here are two more Scriptures about watching our words and our tempers:

- A truly wise person uses few words; a person with understanding is even-tempered (Proverbs 17:27 NLT).
- Don't sin by letting anger control you. Think about it overnight and remain silent (Psalm 4:4 NLT).

WHEN YOUR COACH GETS MAD AT YOU

If a ruler's anger rises against you, do not leave your post; calmness can lay great offenses to rest.
Ecclesiastes 10:4

WARM-UP

How do you respond when someone gets angry with you? Do you fight back or shut down? Feel defensive or discouraged?

"Wrong way, Johnson! What are you *doing*?"

Kara heard her coach yelling something, but she kept sprinting down the court. She had a clear path—that layup was *hers*.

"Wrong basket, Johnson! *Turn around!*"

Realization hit, hard and humiliating: Kara was dribbling toward the wrong basket. The direction had switched at the end of the quarter, and she'd gotten confused.

Cheeks burning, Kara turned to dribble the other way, only to have the ball stolen.

Coach benched her moments later, so angry she wouldn't even make eye contact. Kara put a towel over her head, wishing the court would swallow her up so she could disappear.

We all make mistakes in sports—sometimes embarrassing ones. And passionate coaches may temporarily lose their minds in the middle of a tense play. They may yell at you, embarrass you, bench you. It's no fun being on the receiving end of a coach's fury.

We've seen how the book of Ecclesiastes offers realistic wisdom for a variety of practical life situations. Today's verse offers advice for times when a "ruler," or authority figure, gets mad at us. Solomon says, "Do not leave your post; calmness can lay great offenses to rest."

How do you respond when a coach singles you out for criticism? It can be tempting to fight fire with fire, to push back by defending ourselves or yelling. Or maybe to stomp off in a sulky huff. Maybe we take out our embarrassment and frustration on teammates or family. Or we take the quiet route, shutting down and becoming insecure, making even more mistakes because we're upset.

Solomon's advice offers us a wiser way to handle tense, tricky moments: Stay calm and stay put. Don't run, stomp, stalk, or walk away. Listen to what your coach has to say.

By staying calm, you give your coach (or whoever is angry) a chance to calm down. You show them that you're acting with maturity, not fighting back or falling apart. When we give angry people space, we give them time to cool off. From there, we may get a chance to speak up if needed, or the whole thing may blow over.

If you're ever on the receiving end of a coach's anger, stay cool, stay calm, and say a prayer. Ask God for help and resolution. Then wait for him to help things settle down.

DRILL

Describe a time when showing an angry person patience and grace paid off.

DEALING WITH DIFFICULT PEOPLE

"You have heard the law that says, 'Love your neighbor' and hate your enemy. But I say, love your enemies! Pray for those who persecute you! In that way, you will be acting as true children of your Father in heaven. For he gives his sunlight to both the evil and the good, and he sends rain on the just and the unjust alike. If you love only those who love you, what reward is there for that?"
Matthew 5:43–46 NLT

WARM-UP

Do you find it difficult to practice forgiveness?
Why or why not?

I knew the look on my friend's face. "Bad practice?"

She grunted. Translation: *The worst. Don't ask.*

I waited, knowing she'd spill when she was ready.

"It's Coach Bradley," she said, the name twisting angrily out of her mouth. "He acts like he hates the entire team, especially me."

"I'm sorry," I said, at a loss for how to help.

Sports bring out the best in some people—and the worst in others. Maybe you have a coach, teammate, or opponent who is difficult to deal with. Maybe it feels like they have it out for you, like they enjoy making your sports life miserable.

Jesus was no stranger to dealing with difficult people. Many individuals were offended by his radical inclusion, forgiveness, and zeal. They questioned, criticized, opposed, and mocked him—and Jesus always responded with courage, wisdom, and grace. His example teaches us how to respond to the difficult people in our lives.

In Matthew 5, Jesus begins the Sermon on the Mount by calling his followers to a higher standard of love. He reminds us that it's easy to love people who love us and treat us kindly. It's no struggle to love a teammate like Ellie, who prayed with Alexis when she felt anxious.

But the true test of our love is when we encounter an "enemy"—a challenging person like Coach Bradley.

Jesus reminds us to imitate the heart of the Father, who shows love to both the evil and the good. And thank goodness God does that—even Christians need grace, and God offers it every time.

We find the key to loving and forgiving our enemies, aka difficult people, in these six words: "Pray for those who persecute you." We can take our hurt, confusion, and frustration to God in prayer. We can pray for—and about—the Coach Bradleys in our lives. We can ask God to soften their hearts and change their behavior. We can ask for wisdom and compassion in our interactions.

When we do that, several things happen:

- Prayer provides peace. Now we know that God is aware of the situation.
- Prayer activates our compassion. We realize our "enemy" may be hurting others because they are hurting inside.
- Prayer renews our trust in God's wisdom. We remember that God is working on the other person even when we can't see it.
- Prayer invites God's guidance if we need to seek help or relief from an unhealthy situation.

Satan divides people; Jesus brings us together. And prayer is a powerful weapon against bitterness. We may feel powerless to change the Coach Bradleys in our lives, but we aren't. We can pray for them—and that's the most powerful thing we could possibly do.

TAKE A KNEE

Father, I am struggling in a relationship right now. I feel hurt, confused, and frustrated. Please show me if there's anything I need to do or to change. Please help the other person to control their anger and treat me differently. Please pave the way for forgiveness and resolution. In Jesus's name, amen.

WHEN YOU HAVE SUCCESS (AND A TEAMMATE DOESN'T)

Rejoice with those who rejoice; mourn with those who mourn. Live in harmony with one another. Do not be proud, but be willing to associate with people of low position. Do not be conceited.
Romans 12:15–16

WARM-UP

What makes you feel celebrated by your friends?

Hadley scanned the all-conference lists posted online. First team: Nope. *I didn't expect first team anyway—but yay, Ava made it.* Second team: Her eyes zipped through the names. *Not me, not me—wait . . . me!* There was her name, third from the top, in the most beautiful black sans serif font. *Second team all-conference!*

Joy and adrenaline zipped through her veins. *Wait till I tell Grandma.* She took a screenshot of the list, then scanned it for her friend Josie's name. First team—no Josie. Second team—no Josie. Honorable mention, maybe? No Josie.

Hadley's heart sank. Conflicting emotions warred inside: Disappointment for Josie. Excitement for herself. Uncertainty about how to greet Josie at practice later. Was it okay to be happy? Should she tell Josie she was sorry? Pretend the lists didn't exist?

There's no handbook for How to Be a Good Friend When You Succeed and Your Friend Gets Left Behind—but there really should be. This awkward dynamic happens to sports friends all the time. All. The. Time.

We don't have a sports handbook, but we do have a life handbook—the Bible. And today's verse helps us navigate complicated times in friendships. In a letter to Christians in Rome, Paul reminds us to share one another's burdens and joys: "Rejoice with those who rejoice; mourn with those who mourn."

The best thing we can do in tricky situations is simply empathize with our friends. If a friend is feeling stressed or overwhelmed, we can pray with her like Ellie and Alexis did. If a friend is bummed about a bad performance or missed opportunity, we can sit with her. Listen to her. Hand her tissues and chocolate. Sometimes it helps to assure an overlooked friend that we see her contributions and respect her effort. We can't fix or change the situation, but we *can* show her we care.

Paul adds to his advice: "Do not be proud, but be willing to associate with people of low position. Do not be conceited." When we experience success, let's remain humble and considerate. Wise with our words. Careful not to make a friend feel left out or less than.

Everybody's timeline is different. Everybody has moments when they feel celebrated and times when they feel overlooked. But our friendships can survive these awkward moments if we treat each other with respect and consideration, mourning and rejoicing together.

PRACTICE

Who sometimes gets overlooked on your team? What can you do to make her feel appreciated this week?

WHEN A TEAMMATE HAS SUCCESS (AND YOU DON'T)

I am filled with joy at his success. He must become greater and greater, and I must become less and less.
John 3:29–30 NLT

WARM-UP

How do you celebrate your friends when they succeed?

"Okay, ladies, it's time to announce the roster for the big track meet—I can only take five runners per event, so this was a hard decision."

High School Me waited, breath held, as Coach rattled off names. I clapped and whooped for each name, praying I'd get to clap and whoop for myself too.

Down the list he went, till only one spot remained.

"Cat!"

The name was a two-edged sword, bringing both joy and pain: Joy for my sweet friend Cat, who trained like a beast and completely deserved a spot on the roster, and pain because—well, I wasn't Cat. I wasn't going to the meet.

How do you respond when a friend has success, but you're struggling? Like Alexis, we may feel insecure, afraid that we're falling behind or letting our team down. And as much as we want to be the friend who celebrates others without feeling the tiniest inkling of jealousy, the struggle is real.

When I'm tempted by jealousy, I draw inspiration from John the Baptist. John was a powerful prophet called to prepare the way for Jesus's message. For a while, John had tremendous influence, drawing huge crowds. But when Jesus began his ministry, Jesus's preaching was electric, his success astonishing—and John's ministry was overshadowed.

At first, John's disciples seemed threatened by the new teacher's popularity. They basically said, "Hey, Rabbi, that guy Jesus is baptizing people too, and now everyone is following him instead of you!" (See John 3:26.)

John's response was beautifully humble: "No one can receive anything unless God gives it from heaven." John knew that we all have assignments from God, roles to play. Sometimes God assigns struggle and sacrifice; other times he assigns influence and success. John understood that Jesus's ministry "success" was an assignment from God.

John went on: "He must become greater and greater, and I must become less and less." John understood his role on God's team: He was a supporting player, and Jesus the rising star. (Of course, playing on God's team wasn't about seeking glory or fame—both John and Jesus eventually sacrificed their lives to fulfill God's purposes.)

We can learn from John's attitude when we feel demoted or overlooked. When a teammate or friend achieves the success we've been working and longing for. Those moments test our hearts and our friendships, but John shows us how to respond with wisdom and grace.

John generously expressed verbal support for Jesus, and that's a great starting point for us too. If a friend receives an accolade that you don't, she may feel awkward and even guilty, worried about making you feel left out or left behind. Here's where you can speak up as John did: "I'm proud to be your friend. I am celebrating you so hard!" Words like these reassure your friend that even though you feel disappointed, you are happy for her, and your friendship is safe.

It's okay to feel sad for ourselves and happy for a friend *at the same time*. But like John, we can take joy in our role even if it's different than the one we wanted. We can rejoice with and for friends who succeed, trusting that God is guiding their path—and ours.

DRILL

Send encouraging text messages to a few teammates today.

GOD CARES WHEN YOU LOSE

The LORD is close to the brokenhearted and saves those who are crushed in spirit.
Psalm 34:18

WARM-UP

Who is your go-to person when you need comfort?

Maribel lay in bed, hot tears sliding down her cheeks, pooling in her ears. She didn't even try to wipe them away. She kept replaying that last rally at today's tennis match: the serve, Maribel's return—it was right down the line, perfect. Her opponent's grunt as she miraculously backhanded the ball back. Maribel's own swing. The sound of the ball thwacking into the net. The cheers from the other side as Maribel's supporters groaned in dismay.

And just like that, she'd lost. Game, set, match.

Season over.

No championship, no title.

All her work, all season long, wasted.

All her hopes, all year long, dashed.

She rolled over and cried into her pillow.

Sports don't just break your heart; sometimes they shatter it. When you've spent months, years, preparing for a key game, a big meet, a championship season, failure can feel devastating: *What was the point? Why did I sacrifice so much only to have things end like this?*

In those moments, you may feel deeply alone in your grief. No one can say anything to make you feel better. Some people might accuse you of overreacting, taking sports too seriously. Others might back away, unsure what to say or how to help. They may be trying to give you space, but it makes you feel more isolated than ever. You may feel like no one understands how hard you worked, how much you sacrificed, how devastated you feel. And the truth is, they don't understand. Even though sweet teammates like Ellie can support us by praying with us, no one can step inside our hearts to feel all we feel. No one, that is, but God.

Psalm 34:18 assures us that God draws near when we hurt. When we're heartbroken, he's not intimidated or overwhelmed, inconvenienced or annoyed. He leans in closer. When you feel crushed, like your dreams have died and you'll never be okay again, God is there to help you pick up the pieces. To listen to your cries without interrupting or judging. To cradle you in his ginormous, loving arms. To sit beside you as you grieve. To give you time—because grief takes time—and to remind you in the meantime: *You are loved. You're not alone. And even though you're not okay today, one day you will be okay. And I'm here through it all.*

TAKE A KNEE

Dear Lord, thank you for hurting with me. I don't know how to express all I feel, but thank you for searching my heart and understanding. Thank you for sitting with me in my sadness. In Jesus's name, amen.

WEEKLY CHECK-IN

What went well this week? What was hard? Did I meet the goals I set for myself?

How is my body feeling? How is my heart feeling? How do I feel about my connection with God?

In what ways do I need support? How can I invite that support?

What do I want to pray about for next week? Who can I invite to pray with me and for me?

WEEK 11: REST AND TRUST

Time-Out: My Hopes, Prayers, and Goals for This Week

Broken Arm, Healed Heart: Azurá's Story

A lightning bolt zinged through Azurá's arm—only this lightning flashed on and on and on, an endless storm. Azurá collapsed onto the basketball court.

Hours later, she was headed home. Days later, she was in surgery. Weeks later, she was standing on the sidelines in a cast, watching her team start a new season without her.

At first, all she felt was anger and confusion. Her prayers were filled with questions: *Why did you let this happen to me? Do you not care about my basketball career?*

As time passed, her prayers changed a little. Less asking, more listening. As more time passed, she had unexpected time to think, and rethink, her relationship with basketball. Time she wouldn't have had without the injury.

When the cast came off, the physical therapy began. Painful exercises, but necessary pain. As Azurá worked her arm, day after day, rep after rep, her thoughts wandered: *Why am I playing this sport? What kind of basketball player do I want to be? What kind of teammate? Why does God have me on this team? Am I really stepping into his purposes for me?*

And it wasn't just questions; she also had realizations: *Before the injury, I was in my head a lot: insecure. Tentative. Forcing plays. I want to go back with a different attitude.*

And Azurá experienced another lightning bolt, this one a flash of insight: *I can use this time for more than physical therapy. I can use this time to work on my mindset too.*

Her prayers changed again, asking God to guide her attitude, perspective, and heart. *God, please help me not waste this time. Help me to use it not only to strengthen my arm but to strengthen my attitude and mental game as well.*

Several months later, halfway through the season, Azurá was in the locker room, dressing for her first game back after several months away. Adrenaline hummed through her veins—ah, how she'd missed this feeling. And instead of the anxiety and self-doubt she'd felt throughout last season, she felt excitement. Joy. Gratitude. She wasn't only thankful that she was able to play the game she loved; she was also thankful for the way God had used the last few months to reshape her mindset and relationship with her sport.

As she jogged out to the court, Azurá was amazed to find herself praying a different prayer: *God, thank you for giving me this time to rest and heal and grow. I can't believe I'm thanking you for an injury, but . . . you used it for good. Thank you for loving me enough to give me this time away. You didn't just heal my arm—you also healed my heart.*

WHEN YOU NEED A GENTLE WORD

He tends his flock like a shepherd: He gathers the lambs in his arms and carries them close to his heart; he gently leads those that have young.
Isaiah 40:11

WARM-UP

How do you feel about taking breaks?

In sports, *rest* can feel like a four-letter word. So can *take* and *easy*, as in, "Take it easy." Okay, yes, technically, all those words *are* four-letter words, but you get my meaning: Many athletes view anything rest-related as negative. We might secretly label athletes who rest with another four-letter word: *weak*.

Sometimes we need to hear the no-nonsense voice that says, "Toughen up! Dig deep! Muscle through." Maybe we're feeling sorry for ourselves and it's time to snap out of it. Or we're in a lazy mood and we need a kick in the patootie to get us working hard again.

But other times we need a different voice—a voice that reminds us to be gentle with ourselves. Maybe, like Azurá, we need to take time to heal and then be patient with ourselves as we stumble through physical therapy. Or maybe we're not injured (yet), but we're pushing too hard, and in order to stay healthy we need to (gasp) take it easier at practice. Or perhaps it's time to laugh off a mistake instead of beating ourselves up. Or shrug off a bad performance instead of obsessing over it.

Today's passage from Isaiah 40 offers an affectionate image of God. He loves his people the way a shepherd loves his sheep. He picks up the fuzzy little lambs and carries them in his arms, up against his chest where they can feel his heart beating: *I-love-you-I-love-you-I-love-you. You're-safe-safe-safe*. He gently leads those who need extra care, attention, and time.

This verse echoes Psalm 23, the famous psalm that says, "The LORD is my shepherd... He makes me lie down in green pastures, he leads me beside quiet waters, he refreshes my soul" (vv. 1–3). Take a moment to savor those last four words: "He refreshes my soul." Do you need to be refreshed today? You may be surprised to find, as Azurá did, that a season of rest does good things for both body and soul. Let God's love and kindness replenish your energy and joy, and know that you don't have to prove yourself to him because he already delights in you.

DRILL

Reread today's Scripture several times, letting the words soak deeper into your head and your heart.

WHEN YOU'RE JUST SO TIRED

Do you not know? Have you not heard? The LORD is the everlasting God, the Creator of the ends of the earth. He will not grow tired or weary, and his understanding no one can fathom. He gives strength to the weary and increases the power of the weak. Even youths grow tired and weary, and young men stumble and fall; but those who hope in the LORD will renew their strength. They will soar on wings like eagles; they will run and not grow weary, they will walk and not be faint.

Isaiah 40:28–32

WARM-UP

What does exhaustion look like for you, both physically and mentally?

My girl Cassidy whirled around the kitchen at 6:30 a.m., tossing snacks into her lunch bag, track clothes into a gym bag, and a pile of binders into her book bag.

"Hey, bag lady, what time will you be home from practice?" I asked.

Cassidy half laughed at my dumb joke, then tossed an answer over her shoulder. "Maybe six? But then I have a piano lesson and an AP Lit essay due. I'm so tired, but . . . I can't stop moving."

The sports season can be over-the-top exhausting. You go straight from school to practice to other activities—work, church, clubs—then you finally sit down to do homework. Somewhere in there, you also have to find time to eat dinner, hang out with family and friends, do chores, take a shower . . . your day never stops. *You* never stop.

I first fell in love with today's passage from Isaiah 40 when I was running cross-country my junior year. Like Cassidy, I was taking tough classes, juggling work and church and family commitments, and feeling utterly spent. Like Azurá, I was struggling to find joy in the midst of the pressure and busyness.

Isaiah writes, "Even youths grow tired and weary." *Tired* is a physical feeling—your muscles are worn out, and you could really use a nap. You probably feel tired every day after practice. *Weary* is next-level, deep-down-in-your-bones-not-to-mention-your-heart exhaustion. It's when your *soul* needs a rest.

Midway through the season, most athletes start to feel tired *and* weary. All the grueling weeks of workouts and games and pressure and schedule-juggling start to add up. You may hit a wall physically and emotionally. You may wonder how you'll ever make it to the end of the season. (I hereby pause this devotion for a special announcement: If you feel like you're at a breaking point, please don't be afraid to ask a parent or coach to help you figure out how to get some rest.)

When you're tired and weary, God wants to help. He's never too tired, overwhelmed, or busy to comfort us through *our* exhaustion, overwhelm, and busyness. And consider these words: "Those who hope in the LORD will renew their strength. They will soar on wings like eagles; they will run and not grow weary, they will walk and not be faint."

Somehow, when we hope in God, he gives us the energy we need. The courage to keep flying. The strength to keep going.

If you're feeling exhausted today, first take a break—or a nap if you can. (Our family highly recommends a couch nap under a fuzzy blanket, with the Atlanta Braves quietly being awesome on the TV as background nap-noise.) If you need more rest, ask the people around you for support. And finally, ask God for a dose of his supernatural strength to see you through.

PRACTICE

What's one restful thing you can do this week to take the edge off your tiredness?

____

____

YOU AREN'T FORGOTTEN

Are not five sparrows sold for two pennies? Yet not one of them is forgotten by God. Indeed, the very hairs of your head are all numbered. Don't be afraid; you are worth more than many sparrows.
Luke 12:6–7

WARM-UP

How many hairs do you think you have?

Cassidy looked up from her computer, her expression hurt. "Still no email from the coach. I still don't know if I made the team." Her shoulders slumped. "I bet he forgot about me."

Being forgotten is an awful feeling. An I-must-not-be-very-interesting feeling. An everyone-else-is-more-important-than-me feeling. Perhaps most crushing of all, it's an I-must-not-be-lovable feeling. It's especially easy to feel forgotten when you're forced to take time off like Azurá was: You're doing PT alone while everyone else is bonding at practice, and it seems like they're moving on without you. Even when we know those feelings aren't true, they sometimes *feel* true.

In Luke 12, Jesus used the following example while he was preaching to show his listeners how important they were (and we are!) to God: "Are not five sparrows sold for two pennies? Yet not one of them is forgotten by God . . . You are worth more than many sparrows." In Jesus's day, sparrows were the cheapest birds a person could buy to eat. Jesus's point was this: If God pays attention to the lives of birds that are worth less than half a penny each, *how much more* is he concerned about our precious lives?

Jesus added that God knows the number of hairs on each of our heads. The average human has between 90,000 and 150,000 hairs on their head, depending on how thick each strand is. You and I couldn't count our own hair even if we tried, but God can, *and he does*. He knows how many hairs you wrangle into every cute game-day do.

What does this tell us?

God knows you.

God pays attention—close attention—to you.

God is aware of your needs.

God is actively working in your daily life. Sometimes he protects you from harm altogether and sometimes he allows adversity, but he is still present and working the whole time.

God never forgets about you. Even when he seems silent or his work is happening behind the scenes where you can't see it, he's there.

So go ahead . . . talk to him. Invite him to work in your life. Ask him for his guidance, strength, and help. He's listening, and he cares.

DRILL

How have you seen God at work in your life recently? Has he answered a specific prayer? Encouraged you through a friend? Comforted you after a tough loss?

GOD WANTS TO HEAR YOUR SPORTS PRAYERS

Praise be to the Lord, to God our Savior,
who daily bears our burdens.
Psalm 68:19

WARM-UP

What's easy for you to pray about? What feels less comfortable?

Senior year of high school, a chilly October morning. I sat down to pray before school, my head swimming with stress: friend drama, Calc test, Dad's anxiety, the SAT, finding money for college, that afternoon's sprint workout (I already had anticipatory nausea). I was in a hurry, so I needed to trim my prayer list. *God doesn't want to hear about cross-country,* I told myself. *He wants me to pray about something spiritual or unselfish, like church or friends or family.* So I skipped the sports stuff, prayed about "spiritual" things, and said amen. As I flew out the door in a flurry of books and lunch and running gear, I wondered why I still felt burdened, more anxious than ever.

Sometimes we tell ourselves we should only "bother" God with emergencies, the Major Life Alarms. After all, he has a whole universe to run—planets to spin, gravity to maintain, wars to prevent. But today's Scripture teaches that God is powerful enough (and loving enough) to run the universe *and* support us in daily life.

Today's verse says, "Praise be to the Lord, to God our Savior, who daily bears our burdens" (Psalm 68:19). Those simple words reveal an important truth: God is aware that we have burdens every. Single. Day. Even when we're not going through major drama, we still carry burdens. God cares about them all, including the "little" stressors and the "worldly" struggles, from school to work to friendship to finances to—yep, you guessed it—sports.

I love the way the New Living Translation presents this passage: "Praise the Lord; praise God our savior! For each day he carries us in his arms." God doesn't just lift your burdens *alongside* you, like a friend who takes one corner of a big box you're struggling to carry . . . God carries you too. He lifts you *and* your box.

A beautiful line from 1 Peter 5:7 echoes this message: "Cast all your anxiety on [God] because he cares for you." If something is worrying you, God wants to help you carry it. When we cast a concern on God, we throw it into his arms, and he takes it from there.

Sports are a huge part of your life, and as fun as they are, they are also tremendously stressful. You may face complex relational dynamics with coaches, teammates, and parents. You may struggle to balance schoolwork and your sports schedule. You may face mental, physical, and emotional exhaustion, or a painful injury like Azurá's. All these things weigh on you, worry you. You care about these concerns . . . and God cares about you.

So go ahead, pray about your sport. Pray about your life—*all of it*. God wants to hear, and he's ready to help.

TAKE A KNEE

Father, thank you that you care about my entire life, sports and all. Please help me to carry my burdens this week. In Jesus's name, amen.

WHEN THE FUTURE FEELS SCARY

But I am trusting you, O LORD, saying, "You are my God!" My future is in your hands.
Psalm 31:14–15 NLT

WARM-UP

If you could get a sneak peek at one thing in your future, what would you want to see?

What do you picture when you imagine your future? I can usually picture a few weeks or months ahead, but after that . . . it all gets foggy. So many unknowns. When you're a student athlete, you may have endless questions about your future: *How will the rest of the season go? What will happen next year with my team . . . my coach . . . and me? Will I get to play in college? (Do I even want to play in college?) What career should I pursue?*

If you go too deep down the what's-my-future rabbit hole, you might never come up for air. Psalm 31:14 is a great prayer for times when we're anxious about the future. I admire the way the psalmist, David, so confidently asserts his faith: "I am trusting you, O LORD."

Can I be honest? Those words are hard for me to say. I'm a natural doubter, and I often struggle to believe—really, deep-down-in-my-heart believe—that the future is going to work out. It's not easy for me to hand things over to God and experience a sense of peace. I have to *fight* to find trust and peace. It's helpful to speak those words: "I am trusting you, O Lord." The very act of shaping the words, declaring them aloud, does something good inside. Those words confirm our faith and *tell* our hearts what they need to do and feel.

David goes on to say, "You are my God." What a powerful, simple reminder: God is our God. He is ours . . . and we are his. And then David says, "My future is in your hands." Have you ever tried to picture the hands of God? Psalm 95:4 tells us that God's hands are large enough, powerful enough—and gentle enough—to hold the whole world. And God doesn't just hold the planet—he holds you. You *and* your future.

He's protecting your life, keeping it safe. He knows the deepest parts of who you are, understands you completely—your past, your gifts, your hopes, your dreams, everything that makes you *you* (see Psalm 139). And he keeps all of that in mind as he shapes your future.

If you've been stressing about the future, borrow David's faithful words and speak them to God today. Remember who holds your future safe. You're in the best of hands.

TAKE A KNEE

Dear Father, As Psalm 31:14 says, "I am trusting you, O Lord *. . . You are my God!" My future is in your hands. In Jesus's name, amen.*

GET YOUR HOPES UP

Why, my soul, are you downcast? Why so disturbed within me? Put your hope in God, for I will yet praise him, my Savior and my God.
Psalm 42:11

WARM-UP

What are your biggest hopes for this season?

I hope this is my breakout season.
I hope I hit my goal.
I hope we win the championship.

Hope can be fun: all bubbles and thrills, like your heart is carefree and floating. But hope is also scary, isn't it? If you've ever hoped your heart out (and worked your tail off) for something that *didn't* happen, you know that hope can end in heartbreak. The harder we hope (and work and pray and sweat and bleed), the more devastated we feel if things don't work out. The Bible puts it this way: "The human spirit can endure a sick body, but who can bear a crushed spirit?" (Proverbs 18:14 NLT).

Disappointment is my least favorite feeling. I *despise* it. Sometimes I've tried to sidestep disappointment by avoiding hope altogether. *It's better not to hope at all,* I tell myself. *If I never expect anything good to happen, then I'll never feel disappointed.* That might feel like a "safe" way to live, but it's kind of sad, isn't it?

The pages of the Bible are infused with hope. Today's passage from Psalm 42 reminds us that when we feel downcast and disturbed, it could be that we've put our hope in the wrong place instead of where it belongs: in God.

Are you feeling let down by life or people? Are you feeling disappointed by your body, your coach, your team, or your sport? Is that disappointment stealing your joy? Like Azurá, are you staring down a difficult road, wishing your journey hadn't led you here? When I feel heavy with disappointment, I do a little heart check: *What—or who—am I hoping in? Am I depending on worldly things to bring me joy instead of relying on God?* Hebrews 6:19 tells us that our hope in God is "an anchor for the soul, firm and secure." God is the only source of hope that will never move and never fail.

When your hope is in God rather than your sport, the pressure comes off your performance. When your hope is in God, it means that if you don't achieve a goal, you're disappointed, but you're okay. If you have a rough game (or season), you're sad, but you're okay. Your sport isn't your only hope for happiness and a great future. You remember that God loves you no matter what—win or lose, in shape or out of shape, athlete or artist. When your hope is in God, it's in good hands. So go ahead . . . get your hopes up.

DRILL

Fill in the blanks: If I don't ______________________________,

I'll be okay because ______________________________

____

____

____

____

____

____

____

____

____

____

______________________________.

FINDING PURPOSE IN PAIN

God is our merciful Father and the source of all comfort. He comforts us in all our troubles so that we can comfort others. When they are troubled, we will be able to give them the same comfort God has given us.
2 Corinthians 1:3–4 NLT

WARM-UP

What's your go-to comfort food when you're sad?

Twenty girls sat in a nervous circle on the gym floor. The volleyball coach stood over us, holding a clipboard. "Thanks for coming to tryouts. If I read your name, you didn't make the team and you can head home."

I hugged my bony knees, hoping for a miracle. I'd never played volleyball before, but I loved the game and wanted to learn.

"Elizabeth."

Who knew you could hate the sound of your own name?

I stood up with the other freshman girls who'd been cut. Fifteen pairs of eyes—the eyes of the girls who'd made the team—looked up at us with kind expressions of pity. We forced smiles, squeaked, "Congratulations," and slouched away to call our rides.

Fast-forward years later, and now I'm the mom, sitting with my daughter Cassidy at the kitchen table. She's staring at a basketball roster on her laptop. "My name's not there," she says, swiping a fist at the tears already sneaking out of her eyes. "I thought I'd finally made it. The assistant coach told me I had a great tryout."

I listen to my daughter speak till she runs out of words. My memory flashes back to my volleyball tryout, a miserable memory I'd tried to bury. Unfortunately, I know how Cassidy feels. But fortunately, that means I know what to say—and not say. We both sit at the table and cry.

Pain is . . . well, painful. As an athlete, you'll walk through all kinds of heartaches: The physical pain of injury. The relational pain of feeling left out by teammates. The emotional pain of losses.

In a letter to Christians in Corinth, Paul described the suffering he and his ministry companions were experiencing because of their faith. They were being persecuted, threatened, and mistreated. Yet through every heartache (and body ache!), God's comfort sustained them. And they were determined to turn that blessing around to bless others: "When [others] are troubled, we will be able to give them the same comfort God has given us."

What pain have you suffered in your sport? An injury or setback like Azurá? A disappointment like Cassidy and me? None of us want to suffer, but suffering deepens us, teaching lessons we can't learn from victory. And Paul suggests that God has another purpose for our pain: The pain we experienced—and the comfort God gave us through it—equips us to comfort others when they are hurting.

That disappointment you faced? Now you can sincerely empathize with friends who are discouraged.

That humiliating mistake you'd rather forget? Now you can offer sympathy and a story that might help a friend laugh through her tears.

That injury you sustained? Now you know how to support a teammate who gets hurt. You know just the right combination of I'm-praying-for-you texts and I-love-you hugs and I'm-your-biggest-fan candy deliveries she's going to need.

God doesn't allow adversity because he's unkind or uncaring. And he doesn't comfort us just so we'll feel better all alone in our room—he knows that one day we'll be able to share his comfort with others.

DRILL

Who can you comfort today?

WEEKLY CHECK-IN

What went well this week? What was hard? Did I meet the goals I set for myself?

How is my body feeling? How is my heart feeling? How do I feel about my connection with God?

In what ways do I need support? How can I invite that support?

What do I want to pray about for next week? Who can I invite to pray with me and for me?

WEEK 12: FOR THE LOVE OF THE GAME

Time-Out: My Hopes, Prayers, and Goals for This Week

I Love This Game: Meg's Story

Meg sat in the dugout, trying to hide all the feelings roiling inside: Frustration. Hurt. Disappointment. Embarrassment. Jealousy. Desperation. *How do I get back out on the field?* She watched a teammate jog out to first base—Meg's position—and had to look away.

Game after game, Meg sat on the bench, wrestling with unruly emotions. Her frustration was affecting everything: Her performance. Her friendships. Her peace of mind. Her schoolwork. Her love of softball, the game she'd adored since she was six.

One night she sat on her bed, praying. Begging God to help her get through this season. She then pulled her Bible off a shelf and started reading. She was struck by a story in John 3, where Jesus was rapidly gaining more followers than another well-known teacher named John the Baptist. John responded with humility: "[Jesus] must become greater; I must become less," he said.

Meg was moved by John's trust in God. Truths started clicking into place, truths Meg had been resisting:

God is in control of my season. If he wants me to play, I'll play.

The only thing I can control is how hard I work. When I work hard, I show God how thankful I am to be playing a sport I love.

Obsessing over results is stealing my peace and joy.

I'm going to honor God by giving my all and enjoying softball every day. That's enough.

Meg went to practice the next day with a new mindset, determined to play unselfishly, for God's glory instead of her own. She poured everything she had into warm-ups, batting practice, and drills. For the first time all season, she didn't spend the entire practice stressing over mistakes, comparing herself to teammates, and worrying about what coaches were thinking.

With her mind free to focus on the work, Meg felt the spark of an almost-forgotten emotion: joy. She started to remember all the things she loved about this sport:

The zing in her arms as her bat connected with a pitch.

The slap of the ball hitting her glove.

The laughter with teammates between drills.

In the coming weeks, she clung to her new attitude, giving her best effort but letting God worry about the results. She started going early to practices, putting in extra time. After a few weeks, other girls started joining her, showing up early to mingle their joy and effort with hers. The whole team was having more fun.

But then one day during a session with her hitting coach, Meg got frustrated again. Her batting was still off. She felt discouragement sneaking back into her heart, and that scared her. "I don't want to go backward," she told her coach. "I don't want to feel mad and sorry for myself all the time."

"Your attitude is totally different," her coach said. "Just because you aren't hitting well today doesn't mean you haven't grown as a person and a player."

His reassurance helped Meg kick discouragement aside. *I am different. God has changed me. My hitting today isn't what counts—what counts is working hard to honor God. Success or no success, I love this game. A rough day at practice can't take that gift from me.*

"You're right," Meg said. "Let's hit some more."

YOU MAKE GOD HAPPY

For the Lord your God is living among you. He is a mighty savior. He will take delight in you with gladness. With his love, he will calm all your fears. He will rejoice over you with joyful songs.
Zephaniah 3:17 NLT

WARM-UP

What's your favorite thing about your sport?

My favorite-ever movie line is from *Chariots of Fire*, a film based on the life of Eric Liddell, a Scottish missionary and brilliant runner who won a gold medal in the 1924 Olympics. In the movie, Eric's sister begs him to return to serve on the mission field in China. Eric promises that he will—but first he has a lot of running to do. He says, "I believe God made me for a purpose: for China. But he also made me fast. And when I run, I feel his pleasure."

That line paints a delightful picture in my mind: God, up in heaven, carefully knitting together your body and soul before you were born (see Psalm 139:13–18). He turns to Jesus and says, "I'm giving this girl the Scorching Speed Gene—one day she's going to fly down the track!" Or maybe he says, "I'm giving her the Brilliant Hand-Eye Coordination Gene. When she picks up a ball—any kind of ball—just look out." Father and Son share a gleeful grin.

What joy God took in making you *you*, blessing you with your unique personality and gifts. When you use those gifts, you make God happy. His heart swells with fatherly pride. Today's verse reflects this truth. The prophet Zephaniah foretells a day when Israel's disgrace and suffering will end and God will restore joy to his people. On that day, God will rejoice over them: "He will take delight in you with gladness," Zephaniah promises. "With his love, he will calm all your fears. He will rejoice over you with joyful songs."

If you're a perfectionist like me, you may be painfully aware of all the ways you fall short. In your faith walk, you may worry, *I bet God's disappointed in me. He probably wishes I were stronger and more faithful.* In sports, you might think, like Meg did at first, *Fun? What fun? I'll have fun after I win my position and start hitting my goals. Sports is about improving, and I have a million miles to go.*

Let this passage in Zephaniah encourage you today: Even when we have room to grow, God applauds our efforts. He rejoices with us and over us. Like a proud father, he's up in heaven cheering, thrilled to watch us discover and explore our talents. He didn't give you athletic inclinations just so you'd win games or set records or get a college scholarship—he wanted to enrich your life and give you joy.

Today, why not follow Meg's example and take a moment to simply savor the sport you love? Marvel at the way God has empowered and equipped your body. Remember how fun it is—how satisfying it is—to throw a ball, score a goal, make an assist, master a skill, work in sync with a teammate.

Lean into joy, and remember that God is watching, his heart swelling with yours. Maybe he's elbowing Jesus, saying, "I love the way she loves her game. That's my girl."

TAKE A KNEE

Father, thank you that I am healthy enough and strong enough to play my sport. Thank you for giving me the strength and skills I need, and for allowing me the chance to play. Today, I'm determined to simply enjoy the game. In Jesus's name, amen.

A GOOD DAY FOR A GOOD DAY

This is the day the Lord has made. We will rejoice and be glad in it. Please, Lord, please save us. Please, Lord, please give us success.
Psalm 118:24–25 NLT

WARM-UP

How would you finish this sentence? I'll be happy in my sport when

____.

I'll finally be happy when . . .
we have a winning record.
I set a new PR.
I hit my goal.

What comes after your *when*? What is keeping you from happiness this season?

There's nothing wrong with having goals or pushing ourselves, but as Meg learned, when we refuse to be happy *while* we're chasing our goals, we spend most of our time feeling unhappy or frustrated. That pesky word *when* puts conditions on our happiness. It forces us to constantly postpone joy. We put our heads down and grind, promising ourselves, *The day to feel happy might come eventually, but today is not that day. No, ma'am, no happiness for you! You haven't earned the right to be happy yet!*

Today's passage from Psalm 118 offers a different perspective. It teaches us how to live with unmet hopes and real joy *at the same time*. First, the psalmist says, "This is the day the Lord has made. We will rejoice and be glad in it." He pauses and notices the gift of today: God made this day, gave us this day—a day to laugh, to play, to love. And the psalmist is determined not to waste God's gift: "*We will* rejoice and be glad." He chooses joy, sets his mind to be present and grateful.

But choosing joy doesn't mean the psalmist has a perfect life.

His next lines reveal that, like us, he is living with unmet dreams and unanswered prayers. He is living in between blessings, still longing for success. So even though he has already decided to be happy today, in the next breath he begs God for help: "Please, LORD, please save us. Please, LORD, please give us success."

What a helpful example for us: Instead of saying, "I can only be happy when I have everything I want," this writer has decided to rejoice even when life isn't perfect. Meg embraced that perspective when she decided to enjoy training even when she wasn't getting the results she wanted. You and I can choose the same *even when* attitude.

We can be joyful *even when* things aren't going our way.

We can enjoy being on a team *even when* we don't have the role we want.

We can enjoy working hard *even when* our goals feel far away.

We can enjoy today's blessings *even when* we're praying about tomorrow's problems.

Tomorrow isn't here yet—we only have today. This practice. This game. This meet. And today is a gift from God: Today you get to play on a team. Today you get to be an athlete. Today you get to push yourself and learn new things.

It's a good day for a good day, don't you think?

DRILL

Finish this sentence: I can enjoy my sport this season *even when*

____

____

____

____

____.

HOW TO PARTY WITH GOD

Mary responded: "Oh, how my soul praises the Lord. How my spirit rejoices in God my Savior! For he took notice of his lowly servant girl, and from now on all generations will call me blessed. For the Mighty One is holy, and he has done great things for me."
Luke 1:46–49 NLT

WARM-UP

What's your go-to celebration song?

Jesus's mother, Mary, had just received a surprising visit (and by "surprising visit," we mean "a mind-blowing, faith-bending, life-will-never-be-the-same-again visit") from the angel Gabriel. Mary was going to be a mother. And it wasn't just any baby she was carrying—her baby was the Son of God. Talk about a curveball. *Surprise* doesn't begin to cover all that Mary must have felt.

Mary could have viewed Gabriel's announcement as a somber responsibility or an unwanted burden, but no—she viewed it as the greatest blessing of her life. (I suspect this faithful attitude was one reason God chose Mary to be Jesus's mother!) Mary celebrated Gabriel's news with a song of praise.

Mary's song is one of several celebratory songs women sang in Scripture. In Exodus 15, after the Israelites miraculously crossed the Red Sea to escape slavery in Egypt, Moses's sister Miriam led singing and dancing all along the water's edge. In 1 Samuel 1, when Hannah gave birth to a son after years of infertility, she sang a prayer of thanks to God.

Throughout the Bible, we see God's people taking time to acknowledge victories. They sing, pray, dance, praise, and throw epic parties. God even establishes annual celebrations *requiring* the entire nation of Israel to commemorate certain triumphs over and over again, year after year. The message is clear: It's healthy and godly to celebrate God's blessings.

How do you celebrate your victories? Or perhaps we should back up a step and ask, *Do* you celebrate victories? When something good happens, do you let yourself savor the moment before moving on to the next thing? When you reach one goal, do you pause to rejoice before setting a new one? As Meg learned to do, can you find joy in small improvements even while you're praying for a big breakthrough?

Celebration is an essential part of life and sports. Why is it so important? First, it inspires gratitude. You probably prayed about whatever goal you had—maybe for weeks, months, even years—so it's appropriate to thank God when he answers our prayers with a glorious yes. Celebration also provides an opportunity to thank the people who have supported us in reaching our goals.

Celebration does many other good things for our souls: It acknowledges milestones so we don't overlook our progress. It keeps us inspired, protecting us from discouragement. It gives our hearts rest from nonstop striving. It keeps us humble, reminding us how far we've come and all the people who have helped us along the way.

The next time a good thing happens in life or sports, take time to celebrate, first with God, then with others. As Mary did, thank God for paying attention to your life: "He took notice of this lowly servant girl." As Mary did, thank him for blessing you: "Oh, how my soul praises the Lord!" As Mary did, give the glory to God: "He has done great things for me."

Victories don't come along all the time, so when they do, let's enjoy them to the fullest. And let's invite God to the party.

PRACTICE

Imagine a celebration for your next victory, big or small. Will you go somewhere fun or party at home? Who do you want to celebrate with you? And (because party food is the best kind of food) what will you eat?

___

___

WHY YOU'RE AN MVP

But our bodies have many parts, and God has put each part just where he wants it. How strange a body would be if it had only one part! Yes, there are many parts, but only one body. The eye can never say to the hand, "I don't need you." The head can't say to the feet, "I don't need you." In fact, some parts of the body that seem weakest and least important are actually the most necessary.
1 Corinthians 12:18–22 NLT

WARM-UP

When do you feel most valuable to your team?

"Great game," I told my girl Avery. "The defense made a huge difference in this win."

She grinned. "Thanks. I'm proud of us."

"You all deserved some loudspeaker shout-outs, but . . ." I didn't finish the sentence. Avery knew what I was going to say: *But they only announce the names of players who score or assist goals.*

Avery shrugged with a who-cares smile. "It's okay. We don't need an announcer to tell us we're valuable."

Most sports have glamorous positions that get a lot of airtime and press. While other roles are just as important (and just as difficult), their effort often goes unseen, unnoticed, and uncelebrated.

In 1 Corinthians 12, the apostle Paul compares God's church to a human body, a wonderfully complex creation. Just as our bodies have a staggering number of parts, each playing a specific role, so it is with the church: many parts (people!) are working toward a common purpose. In a similar way, athletic teams bring together multiple players, each making unique contributions toward a unified purpose. Each teammate needs the other, and while some positions may be more visible than others, each role has value.

Maybe you've looked at a different position on your team and thought, *I wish I played that position—it's more important than mine.* Or you've admired a talented teammate and wished, *If only I had her speed... her height... her strength.* In moments when we're tempted to devalue our own role and gifts, like Meg was tempted to do during her difficult season, Paul's words provide an empowering perspective. If you were just like your teammate, then your team would lack *your* gifts, *your* strengths. If every player were built alike, each one possessing the same physicality and skill sets, then your team would be imbalanced and incomplete.

And Paul notes that the quieter, humbler positions can be the most important of all. They may be the foundation supporting the rest of the team. Just as "the eye can never say to the hand, 'I don't need you,'" so every part of an athletic team is essential. The offense can score a gazillion points, but if the defense doesn't pull their weight, you could still lose the game. The flashy players can't do their fancy stuff by themselves. Someone has to assist the dunk, set the pick, protect the goal. Someone has to swim or run the middle leg of the relay.

God gave you gifts and skills, and your team needs them. Your coach put you in your position for a reason, because that's where your team needs you. Your team doesn't need you to be any other player besides yourself.

And consider this: Your greatest contributions may go beyond athleticism. Maybe you offer encouragement, friendship, or leadership. Maybe you are the glue holding your team together. Whatever your gifts and your role, your team needs you to offer them with confidence and joy.

PRACTICE

What do you bring to your team that no one else does?

____

____

____

RESULTS AREN'T EVERYTHING

The seventy-two returned with joy and said, "Lord, even the demons submit to us in your name." He replied, "I saw Satan fall like lightning from heaven . . . However, do not rejoice that the spirits submit to you, but rejoice that your names are written in heaven."
Luke 10:17–18, 20

WARM-UP

What's the best loss you've ever experienced?

I recently spotted a friend in the grocery store, and we stopped to chat. "Your daughter made the new flag football team, didn't she? How is her first season going?" I asked.

Lordes thought for a minute. "Well, last week was weird. Her team lost a game that felt like a win, and they won a game that felt like a loss. Does that make sense?"

"Absolutely."

If you know what Lordes meant, then you understand an important truth about sports: Results aren't everything. The win-loss column isn't everything. Winning is only part of the equation. Sometimes progress—and process—are even more important.

In Luke 10, Jesus sent seventy-two of his disciples out to preach the Good News and prepare the way for his ministry. As they went, the disciples healed people and drove out demons, using special gifts Jesus had given them for the missionary journey. When the disciples returned, they seemed especially excited about the whole we-got-to-drive-out-demons part. (To be fair, who wouldn't be?) Jesus rejoiced with them, but then he cautioned them not to focus too much on results: "Do not rejoice that the spirits submit to you, but rejoice that your names are written in heaven."

Jesus reminded them that some things are more important than others—more lasting than others. Performing miracles was cool, but going to heaven to be with God forever was the greatest miracle of all. Jesus's disciples could rejoice in their salvation every day, no matter how their earthly ministry was going.

In a similar way, the win-loss column isn't the only measure of success. Maybe your record isn't great, but your team is having a breakthrough year in selfless play. Maybe the other team won, but your team finally put together some complex plays. Maybe the other team scored more points, but your team exhibited greater sportsmanship.

When you don't get the win or hit the goal you wanted, that doesn't automatically make the day a loss. Resilient athletes ask themselves, "What victories *can* I celebrate?" Like Meg, they focus on the things they can control, like their effort and attitude. They identify progress and milestones along the way. They notice the moments of triumph hiding inside defeats.

As Christians, we can take Jesus's lesson even deeper: As daughters of God, we have eternal blessings that will far outlast any trophy or title. Maybe to your teammates, winning a championship or setting a record is the greatest joy they could imagine. But Christians are blessed with joys that are so much greater than sports. We have the devoted love of a faithful Father. Forgiveness for every sin. The promise of heaven.

Trophies tarnish. Records get broken and forgotten. But our joy in Christ never rusts or fades, and our inheritance in Christ can never be taken away.

DRILL

Besides earning a winning record, how would you define a winning season for yourself? For your team?

____

____

COMFORT FOR UNANSWERED PRAYERS

Why do you complain, Jacob? Why do you say, Israel, "My way is hidden from the LORD; my cause is disregarded by my God"? Do you not know? Have you not heard? The LORD is the everlasting God, the Creator of the ends of the earth. He will not grow tired or weary, and his understanding no one can fathom. He gives strength to the weary and increases the power of the weak . . . . Those who hope in the LORD will renew their strength.
Isaiah 40:27–29, 31

WARM-UP

What makes you feel insecure with God?

I sat in the bleachers, leaking tears. I could hardly bear to watch. My friend was standing on the sideline, benched. Head bowed, shoulders drooping, heart breaking. This was supposed to be her big chance. Her first start. But she'd made a few mistakes, and the coach pulled her out after ten minutes. Didn't give her another chance.

All week, we'd been praying together, begging God to bless her game and give her the success she'd worked so hard to achieve. The success she deserved (so much more than anyone else on the team, in my completely unbiased, best-friend opinion). Instead, we got this—the exact opposite of everything we'd prayed for.

My thoughts were a blender of doubt-flavored questions: *Why is God letting this happen? Does he not see? Worse, does he not care?*

The disappointment of unanswered prayers can make us insecure. Make us doubt God's power and love. Is he not paying attention? Is he too busy? Does he simply not care? (Or does he not like sports?)

We aren't the first people to question God when life is disappointing or difficult. Scripture depicts many believers who suffered, then asked God why. Today's verse is a poem from the book of

Isaiah, an emotional passage in which people question God and he responds.

God's people complain, "My way is hidden from the LORD." In other words, *God doesn't see or hear me.* And they say, "My cause is disregarded by my God." Or, *God doesn't care about me.*

God responds by turning their questions around: "Do *you* not know? Have *you* not heard?" In other words, *Do you not see and hear what I am doing?* From there, God's response offers hope-filled promises that show how much he loves us. If we let them, these promises set our hearts soaring:

- *"He will not grow tired or weary, and his understanding no one can fathom."* God isn't too tired to pay attention, and his wisdom far surpasses ours. He even sees the future.
- *"He gives strength to the weary and increases the power of the weak."* God doesn't play favorites with fancy people and famous athletes; he also cares about the humble and the unseen.
- *"Those who hope in the Lord will renew their strength."* Hope in God strengthens us.

As Meg reminded herself when her season wasn't going well, *God is in control. If he wants me to play, I'll play.*

When life or sports don't go your way, or prayers go unanswered and the enemy whispers doubt into your heart, take your questions to God. Circumstances change, but his love never does. It never fades and never fails. We can depend on it.

TAKE A KNEE

Father, thank you for being trustworthy and loving. Even when I don't understand why you are allowing difficulties in my life, I know you care and want to comfort and strengthen me. My hope is in you. In Jesus's name, amen.

RESILIENT JOY

Rejoice in the Lord always. I will say it again: Rejoice!
Philippians 4:4

WARM-UP

What's your happy place?

My happy place is the beach at sunset. My family sprints ahead of me, laughing and splashing. A light breeze tickles my hair. It's just cool enough that I need a hoodie, and the sand feels chilly between my toes. Sunset melts into the water, staining it seashell pink.

Maybe your happy place is cartwheeling off the field with teammates after a win, plotting to go out for victory milkshakes. Or spending summer mornings in the weight room, working hard and dreaming about next season, your nose filled with Eau de High School Gym, that one-of-a-kind smell where rusty metal and ancient rubber meet cheap body spray and decades of teenage sweat—it's mostly gross, but weirdly great.

Paul wrote the book of Philippians as a letter to Christians in Philippi, and it's easily his happiest letter. Its four chapters bubble over with gratitude, hope, and joy—contagious joy. Do you remember where Paul was writing from? He wasn't relaxing on a beach or pursuing athletic glory—Paul wrote his letter from prison.

I don't know about you, but I don't usually sprinkle the world with joy when my life is hard. The worse my life is going, the more mopey and complain-y I become. Not Paul. He could be happy—and *spread* happy—even from jail. We get a clue to the source of Paul's resilient joy when he writes, "Rejoice *in the Lord*." He doesn't say, "Rejoice in life's positive situations. Find joy in athletic success, good grades, easy friendships, and fun plans." No—Paul urges us to rejoice *in the Lord*.

The Lord is the only reliable constant in our lives. Our circumstances can change day to day, sometimes minute by minute. (Ever had an awesome game or race fall apart in the last sixty seconds?) If our joy depends on our circumstances, then we're riding an emotional roller coaster. As Meg discovered, if our joy depends on how our athletic season is going—or how each workout or competition is going—well, that roller coaster is probably giving us whiplash.

When we draw joy from the Lord, it means:

- Our joy doesn't depend on a practice or game.
- It doesn't depend on a coach's approval.
- It doesn't depend on your performance or record.

Our joy depends on who God is, and he is always good. Always kind. Always with us and for us.

When God is our source of joy, then our joy is resilient. It's bad-game proof, injury proof, moody-teammate proof, losing-record proof. We can find joy anytime, anywhere, because *God* is our happy place.

PRACTICE

List some ways God brings you joy.

1. ______________________________

____

____

____

2. ______________________________

____

____

____

3. ______________________________

____

____

____

WEEKLY CHECK-IN

What went well this week? What was hard? Did I meet the goals I set for myself?

____

____

____

How is my body feeling? How is my heart feeling? How do I feel about my connection with God?

____

____

____

In what ways do I need support? How can I invite that support?

____

____

____

What do I want to pray about for next week? Who can I invite to pray with me and for me?

____

____

____

Time-Out: My Hopes, Prayers, and Goals for the Offseason

WHEN YOU'RE REALLY, REALLY (REALLY) HOPING FOR SOMETHING

Many are the plans in a person's heart, but it is the LORD's purpose that prevails.
Proverbs 19:21

WARM-UP

What's your number one sports prayer right now?

Tryouts were over. Lane had nothing left to do but wait and wonder: *Did I perform well enough? Strike the right balance between standing out but also playing selflessly?*

For a half second she imagined herself making the team: *First I'll scream. And then—the look on Dad's face when I tell him!* Hope rose—and so did nausea.

She tried to kill the hope before it took a first breath. *Quit fantasizing, Lane, you'll jinx it!*

Now she felt a different kind of nausea—a my-life-is-over-if-I-don't-make-this-team nausea. *That dream of playing in college? Forget it. Everything rides on this. One. Decision.*

Every athlete has make-or-break moments where it feels like their entire future is on the line. Will you make the team? Make the next round of playoffs? Get the call from the college coach? In those moments, it can be difficult to think clearly. Difficult even to imagine a different path than the one your heart is set on. And trusting God with the outcome? Way harder than it sounds.

Complicated times call for simple truths like Proverbs 19:21: "Many are the plans in a person's heart, but it is the LORD's purpose that prevails." Maybe your plans and dreams are so big you're afraid to speak them aloud in case someone laughs or tells you to get over yourself.

It's exciting to have plans and dreams. What's the fun in life if we never reach for challenging things? God welcomes our wildest-dream prayers, and he loves to hear the longings of our hearts. But as hard as we hope and as desperately as we beg God to say yes to our desires, the second part of today's verse keeps our faith rooted in a key truth: "It is the LORD's purpose that prevails."

That thought is both encouraging and sobering. It's encouraging because it means nothing can stand in the way of God's plans for your life. If God wants you to make a team, you're going to make the team. No player, coach, mistake, or misfortune can stand in your way.

It's sobering because it means we must accept God's plans for our lives even when they're different from ours. Romans 8:28 assures us, "In all things God works for the good of those who love him, who are called according to his purpose." If you don't make the team . . . get the call . . . get the win . . . God is working for your good even through the disappointment. God has good in store for you somehow, some way, even if you can't see it right now.

God is working through whatever big decision or outcome you're waiting on today. He sees your desires, hears your prayers, and he is thoughtfully weighing what is best. Cling to that truth. It may not take away all your nerves, but it can ease your fears and help you trust as you wait, hope, and pray.

TAKE A KNEE

Dear Father, thank you for wanting what is best for me and knowing what is best for me. Thank you for caring about my desires and dreams. Please give me peace as I wait, and help my heart to truly trust yours. In Jesus's name, amen.

GAME-DAY DEVOTION #1: IT'S NOT ALL UP TO YOU

The horse is made ready for the day of battle,
but victory rests with the LORD.
Proverbs 21:31

WARM-UP

What food turns your stomach on game days? What settles your stomach when you're nervous?

It was the morning of the big race. I'd been training my heart out (not to mention my legs and lungs), and this afternoon's race would be my last chance to qualify for the conference meet in the 1600-meter run.

Before breakfast, I sat on my bed trying to read my Bible, but I was barely able to think straight. A light tap sounded at my door, and Dad popped his head in.

"Hey, Sweetie, how are you feeling?"

"Haven't thrown up yet, but getting close."

Dad flashed his crinkle-eyed smile. "Can I read you a verse that might help?"

"Sure."

Dad sat on the end of my bed and read, "The horse is made ready for the day of battle, but victory rests with the LORD."

"So you're saying I'm a horse?"

Dad laughed. "I'm saying you've prepared for your battle—your race—the best you can, and now the outcome rests with God."

I've read this verse a million times since then, anytime I'm waiting for an outcome that isn't entirely under my control. This verse reminds me that I'm in charge of preparation, but the ultimate victory isn't up to me. It's up to God.

To be fair, this proverb was not originally written about sporting events. It was speaking about war, not athletics. However, the larger principle we find in this verse still helps to settle our minds when we're biting our fingernails over significant outcomes: *Will we get the win? Will we make the playoffs?* The reminder that "victory rests with the LORD" takes the pressure off our performance because the results aren't *only* up to us. Our job is to get the metaphorical horse ready for battle—to train, condition, practice, prepare. After that, our job is to trust God—and *his* job is to take it from there. God determines the end result.

No matter the outcome, you're in good hands—God's hands. He knows what you need to be happy and to live the life he wants for you. He loves you, win or lose.

Now get out there and have fun playing your heart out—it's game day.

PRACTICE

Today as you play, remind yourself: I love this game. Win or lose, I'm glad I get to play the sport I love.

GAME-DAY DEVOTION #2: SIMPLE TRUTHS FOR GAME DAYS

And I am convinced that nothing can ever separate us from God's love. Neither death nor life, neither angels nor demons, neither our fears for today nor our worries about tomorrow—not even the powers of hell can separate us from God's love. No power in the sky above or in the earth below—indeed, nothing in all creation will ever be able to separate us from the love of God that is revealed in Christ Jesus our Lord.
Romans 8:38–39 NLT

WARM-UP

What truth do you need to remember about God today?

On game days, thoughts fly around my head like baby tornados in a blender. I can hardly hold a conversation, let alone a series of rational, spiritual thoughts. I have to cling to one simple idea at a time.

Here are some simple truths you can cling to on game days. Each one is inspired by today's passage from Romans. If anxious thoughts are whirling around your brain today, I invite you to choose one or two of these truths as your focus for the day:

- God loves me.
- God pays close attention to my life.
- God hears my prayers.
- God knows this competition is important to me.
- God cares about my health, my happiness, and my future.
- God cares about my sport, but he cares even more about my heart, my holiness, and my walk with him.
- If I win, it's a blessing from God, and I will turn the victory into praise.

- If I lose, God is still with me, and I will trust and praise him through my disappointment.
- If I lose, it doesn't mean God is angry with me, against me, or punishing me.
- If I win, God will help me to stay humble and handle success.
- If I lose, God will see me through the challenges of heartache, confusion, and disappointment.
- I am a daughter of God, and no game (no anything) can change that.
- Win or lose, I will go to bed tonight completely loved by my Father in heaven.

PRACTICE

Choose one of these truths as your thought for the day. Repeat it to yourself whenever wild worries try to knock you off your feet. This thought can serve as a spiritual lifeline, keeping you connected to God and grounded in his love.

A DEVOTION FOR THE DAY AFTER A TOUGH LOSS

You keep track of all my sorrows. You have collected all my tears in your bottle. You have recorded each one in your book.
Psalm 56:8 NLT

WARM-UP

What bothers you most about losing?

My basketball team had lost the county championship by two points. One basket. I was so devastated and angry, I could hardly speak on the ride home. At home I hid in my room, fuming, replaying every fail. *How'd I miss that easy layup? It would have tied the game!*

Hours later, my dad got home. He sat on the end of my bed, empathy radiating from his warm brown eyes. "I'm so sorry," he said. "I hate to lose too."

His words brought my guard down, and I finally started speaking.

I vented, ranted, and cried. Dad listened, listened, and listened some more.

An hour later, I was exhausted, but a little less mad. A little less sad. Because I'd been heard by someone who got it. My grief had been witnessed.

You may not have a sympathetic earthly dad who will sit and hear you out after a loss, but you do have a heavenly Father who cares deeply about your life. Drink in the comfort in these words, which the psalmist wrote as a prayer to God: "You keep track of all my sorrows. You have collected all my tears in your bottle. You have recorded each one in your book."

What does it mean for God to keep track of your sorrows? It means if you are hurting, he is the first to know. No tear you shed ever goes unwitnessed. No cry goes unheard, no heartache unshared.

The Bible affirms our experience with sorrow, validating the crushing, confusing experience of heartache. Psalm 34:18 says, "The

Lord is close to the brokenhearted and saves those who are crushed in spirit."

When you are brokenhearted, watching your dreams and hopes drift limply to the ground like wilting balloons, God leans in close. He steps in to let you cry on his shoulder and hold you safe in his arms.

As heartbroken as you feel today, joy can come again. *Will* come again. Psalm 30:5 reminds us, "Weeping may stay for the night, but rejoicing comes in the morning." A new day may bring new hope and fresh joy. But for now—today, tonight—if your heart is broken, let it be. Sit with your Father and cry it out. He's listening.

PRACTICE

If you can't find the words to pray, try writing your thoughts and feelings down like a letter to God.

A DEVOTION FOR CELEBRATING A VICTORY

Then Miriam the prophet, Aaron's sister, took a tambourine and led all the women as they played their tambourines and danced. And Miriam sang this song: "Sing to the LORD, for he has triumphed gloriously; he has hurled both horse and rider into the sea."
Exodus 15:20–21 NLT

WARM-UP

What's your favorite way to celebrate a win?

God's people, the Israelites, had just experienced an astounding series of events. God had sent plagues to convince the Egyptians that enslaving the Israelites (and angering their God) was a horrible idea. He'd sent frogs and gnats (gross), boils and blood (double gross), disease and death (tragic), plus a few more. After all this, the Egyptian pharaoh finally set the Hebrews free, only to change his mind a few days later. He sent his army to chase them down, to drag them back in chains. The Israelites were soon trapped between a savage army and an uncrossable sea.

All night long, God blew the sea back, back, back. Up it piled, a heaving wall of water held in place by an invisible hand, making a way for God's people to walk across. The Egyptians followed in fierce pursuit. Two million Israelites—men, women, children, livestock—began the crossing, rushing and terrified. *Hurry, hurry, don't look back, don't listen to the pounding of the hooves, the shouting of the soldiers drawing closer, ever closer. Hurry, hurry, get to the other side.*

The moment the last Israelite set foot on the opposite bank, God pulled back his hand, releasing the pent-up wall of water. It thundered back into place, pummeling the Egyptian army. Burying them in a watery grave.

As the Israelites stood safe on the far shore, gaping in awe at this, the greatest (so far) of God's mighty miracles, a woman named Miriam stepped up to lead a celebration. Singing, dancing, tambourines, praise—Miriam led a conga line before the world had heard of conga lines.

God loves a party, and he deserves to be praised. The next time you have an epic victory—or any victory—why not invite God to the celebration? It's not ungodly to give full vent to your joy. To dance, sing, shout, and cry with best-day-ever gratitude and glee.

And don't just celebrate one time—take that victory-memory out time after time to taste its sweetness all over again. God called his people to re-celebrate their escape from Egypt every year with a festival called Passover—this tells us it's healthy and godly to relive our victories. To pause life, look back, and say, "Lord, I haven't forgotten what you did—the prayers you answered, the help you gave, the joy you allowed me to experience. Thank you all over again." As time passes, this helps our gratitude to deepen and grow, not dim and fade.

The next time you experience a great win, mark it with a great celebration. Like Miriam, pull out your tambourine—your favorite playlist, your victory jam—and start that conga line. God will be first in line behind you.

DRILL

Make a list of your top three sports victories. Relive those moments in your memory, then relive them in prayer. Thank God for all the ways he came through for you.

1. ____________________

2. ____________________

3. ____________________

A DEVOTION FOR THE END OF THE SEASON: THE ONE WHO CAME BACK

One of them, when he saw that he was healed, came back to Jesus, shouting, "Praise God!" He fell to the ground at Jesus' feet, thanking him for what he had done.
Luke 17:15–16 NLT

WARM-UP

How do you feel when someone thanks you?

At least once a year, I catch my husband, Kevin, hanging up his phone with a sentimental look on his face. "What's going on?" I ask.

"I just called Coach Bobo to tell him how much I appreciate everything he did for me in high school. I am who I am because of him, and I want to make sure he knows I've never forgotten."

And this is one of the reasons I adore my husband: On the outside he looks like an intimidating athlete; on the inside, he's full of grateful warm fuzzies, and he's not afraid to share them.

In Luke 17, we read about an encounter Jesus had with ten men who had leprosy. Leprosy wasn't just a disfiguring skin disease; it also made its victims social outcasts. Victims were usually quarantined, forced to leave their families and live in isolated colonies. The ten sick men approached Jesus, begging for healing.

Jesus told them, "Go show yourselves to the priests" (v. 14), and as they went, they were healed. Their sores disappeared, their pain faded, their skin was restored. Just imagine their amazement, the shouts and tears of joy: They could go home to their families!

One of the lepers stopped, turned, and sprinted all the way back to Jesus, throwing himself at Jesus's feet and praising God. Jesus asked, "Didn't I heal ten men? Where are the other nine?" (v. 17).

Ten had been healed, but only one returned to thank Jesus. I want to be like the man who came back, don't you? A person who always takes time to thank the people who help me. A person who isn't afraid of vulnerability, even if it means I shed a little tear.

As your season nears its close, think about all the people who made it possible: coaches, family members, friends. Before you move on to the next thing—whether that's a restful offseason, a busy travel season, or a new team at the next level—are there people you want to thank for supporting you?

Like the healed man, let's pause and say thank you. Like Kevin, let's make the phone call, send the text, write the card—not just once, but many times. Let's be among the ones who come back.

DRILL

Who do you want to thank for supporting you this season? How would you like to express your gratitude?

ABOUT THE ATHLETES

Author's Note: *I am oh so thankful for the ladies who shared their stories and hearts with us in these pages. As you will see, some of them are athletes who compete casually, and others are elite athletes competing at the highest levels in their sport. Here's a little more about their lives.*

ELENA: MORE THAN THIS SPORT

Elena is still playing on her high school's varsity soccer team and loving every minute. She also volunteers with Beta Club and her youth group. She plans to continue playing in college while also pursuing a nursing degree.

ALLIE: I CALL THAT A WIN

Allie no longer swims competitively, but she still shares her love of swimming by teaching swim lessons at her local pool. She is active in her youth group, leads her school's prayer club, and is an editor for her school newspaper.

JINCY: DRY BONES

Jincy Dunne Roese plays for the New York Sirens of the Professional Women's Hockey League and serves on the PWHL Players' Association. She played for the Ohio State University, was a member of the United States Women's National Ice Hockey Team, and represented the United States at the 2022 Winter Olympics. You can follow her online at @jrdunne33.

HANNAH: WE DID IT

Hannah Grace became the national pole vault champion and the North Carolina all-time high school record holder with a PR of 14'6". She graduated from Coastal Christian High School and went on to vault at the University of Tennessee. She hopes to vault in the Olympics. You can follow her career at @hannahgrace.vaults.

LIBBY: GIVE YOURSELF AWAY

Libby kept fighting for friendships on her team. The summer after graduation, she started hanging out more often with one of her former cross-country teammates, and they grew very close throughout their college years. They were bridesmaids in each other's weddings, and they remain friends today.

MERLOT: LAST CHANCE

Merlot Bader began her gymnastics career when she was eight years old, and she competed all the way through high school. Her first year in college, she competed on the Acrobatics and Tumbling Team at Hawaii Pacific University, where she was a tumbler and a top. Although she is no longer competing, she is still attending HPU, taking hikes around the island with friends, working part-time, and attending a local church.

ANNABELLE: READY OR NOT

Annabelle Hasselbeck was a member of the Boston College women's lacrosse team that won the national championship in 2024. After graduation, she went to work for Sports Spectrum, where she highlights the faith of other Christian athletes on her podcast. You can follow her life and faith at @abhasselbeck.

JAIYA: JUST KEEP TRUSTING

Jaiya Patillo is a national champion, junior Olympian, and the Nebraska state record holder for the women's 400-meter race. She also holds national records for the 400-meter race for multiple age groups. Jaiya strives to glorify God in every race she runs, and she hopes to compete in the Olympics. You can follow her ongoing career at @jaiyapatilloofficial.

EMILY: GOD'S NOT DONE WITH ME

Emily Gillespie stayed to play her senior field hockey season for Boston College. She shone a light for the Lord on her team, and she has no regrets about her decision. After spending a year working in Paris, she went on to attend medical school at the University of Kentucky. You can connect with Emily at @emilygillespie.

ALEXIS: ALL THE FEELS

Alexis Maharty cheered for one year in high school and three years at Duke University. She is now a registered nurse (RN) working on a medical/surgical unit at Duke University Hospital. In her free time, she loves reading sci-fi books and traveling, and she volunteers with her church's campus ministry. You can keep up with Alexis at @alexis_cookie.

AZURÁ: BROKEN ARM, HEALED HEART

Azurá Stevens is a forward for the Los Angeles Sparks. She played high school basketball at Cary High, college basketball at Duke University and the University of Connecticut, and has played in the WNBA since 2018. You can find her on Instagram at @azura_stevens.

MEG: I LOVE THIS GAME

Meghan Schouten is a member of the Boston College softball team. Her faith keeps her grounded and inspired on and off the field. You can follow her life and career on Instagram at @mschouten20.

ACKNOWLEDGMENTS

Publishing books is like sports: It's a team effort. I am deeply thankful for the team of people who devoted time, talents, and prayers to this book.

I couldn't write without the faithful support of family and friends. Kevin, Cassidy, Blake, Avery, and Sawyer, I adore you beyond words. Thank you for letting me share our stories and for showing grace when we eat too much pizza as deadlines approach. Bill and Glenda, thank you for all the help chauffeuring and shopping. Emma, thank you for your faithful check-ins and the last-minute Rescue Edits! Deepest thanks to my agent, Ingrid Beck, who caught the vision from day one and went above and beyond in championing this work.

The team at Zonderkidz has been an absolute joy. Megan Dobson and Katherine Easter, thank you for including me in every step of production. Katherine, thank you for helping shape the devotions so beautifully, helping me find a confident, clear direction. Jacque Alberta, your attention to detail and nuance are superpowers. Thank you for fighting *so hard* to let me keep so many darlings. Abby VanWormer, marketer extraordinaire, your creativity and enthusiasm made marketing so fun! Denise Plant, thank you for translating words like "feisty and feminine" and "gritty and girly" into images, colors, and fonts. Favorite. Cover. Ever. Kristen Sasamoto, the interior design is stunning—I'm still happy-dancing. Ginormous thanks for the Hail Mary design gymnastics that miraculously made All The Things fit! Big thanks to Gabriella Wikidal for managing the cover design, and Mary Hassinger for contributing your eagle eye. Mandi Ogle, I loved working together on the audiobook.

To the athletes and endorsers who lent support and stories to this project (some before the book had even been written): This book wouldn't exist without you. I'm forever thankful.